More Praise
The BUDDHA'S
of LIBERATION

"A clear presentation of the three turnings of the wheel of the Buddha's teachings. James William Coleman draws on textual references in the sutras, his experience in both the Zen and Vajrayana traditions, and his Western academic training to lay out in modern language and with sensitivity to a modern audience this easy-to-read and approachable overview of the Buddhist path and practice."
—Lama Drupgyu Tenzin, vice president of the Tsadra Foundation

"James William Coleman writes with power and precision on a subject of great contemporary importance: the three turnings of the Dharma wheel. This beautifully written meditation on the great sutras is both a succinct explanation of the founding tenets of Buddhism and a profound reflection upon the evolution of those ideas through time. Novices and religious scholars alike will be both taught and inspired by this wonderful book."
—Robert Inchausti, author of *Thomas Merton's American Prophecy*

"This marvelous book offers a pithy, cogent description of the arc of the Buddha's teachings—from *anatta* (non-self) to *shunyata* (emptiness) to *tathata* (buddha nature). James William Coleman provides clear, simple language to describe some of the most complex ideas within the Buddhist canon and offers practical interaction for how to bring those teachings alive in practice and daily life. Chapters by Tenshin Reb Anderson Roshi and Lama Palden Drolma provide a rich invitation into the paths of Zen and Vajrayana. The book is a gem for both beginning and seasoned practitioners."
—Pamela Weiss, founder of Appropriate Response

The BUDDHA'S DREAM *of* LIBERATION

Freedom, Emptiness, *and* Awakened Nature

James William Coleman

with Reb Anderson Roshi
and Lama Palden Drolma

Wisdom

Wisdom Publications
199 Elm Street
Somerville, MA 02144 USA
wisdompubs.org

Library of Congress Cataloging-in-Publication Data

Names: Coleman, James William, 1947– author.
Title: The Buddha's dream of liberation: freedom, emptiness, and awakened nature /
    James William Coleman, with Reb Anderson Roshi and Lama Palden Drolma.
Description: Somerville, MA: Wisdom Publications, 2017. |
    Includes bibliographical references and index.
Identifiers: LCCN 2016044494 (print) | LCCN 2016050995 (ebook) | ISBN
    9781614293583 (pbk.: alk. paper) | ISBN 1614293589 (pbk.: alk. paper) | ISBN
    9781614293750 | ISBN 9781614293750 (ebook) | ISBN 1614293759 (ebook)
Subjects: LCSH: Dharma (Buddhism)
Classification: LCC BQ4190 .C65 2017 (print) | LCC BQ4190 (ebook) |
    DDC 294.3/444—dc23
LC record available at https://lccn.loc.gov/2016044494

ISBN 978-1-61429-358-3   ebook ISBN 978-1-61429-375-0

21 20 19 18 17
5 4 3 2 1

Cover design by Jess Morphew. Interior design by Kristin Goble. Set in Fairfield Light 10.5/15.

Wisdom Publications' books are printed on acid-free paper and meet the guidelines for permanence and durability of the Production Guidelines for Book Longevity of the Council on Library Resources.

This book was produced with environmental mindfulness.
For more information, please visit wisdompubs.org/wisdom-environment.

Printed in the United States of America.

MIX
Paper from
responsible sources
FSC® C005010
www.fsc.org

Please visit fscus.org.

To my teachers, Reb, Toni, Palden, and Rose

And to my muse, Claudia

Publisher's Acknowledgment

The publisher gratefully acknowledges the generous contribution of the Hershey Family Foundation toward the publication of this book.

Contents

Preface

The explosion of interest in mindfulness and meditation practice has brought Buddhist wisdom to a wider audience than ever before. But with all its promise and possibilities for this crisis-torn world, the spread of this new, more-secular form of Dharma also brings the danger that we may lose sight of the tradition's deepest, most profound teachings.

There is, I think, no better way to avoid that danger than to study the classic sutras, and that is what this book is all about. Even though most people find them pretty intimidating at first, to read them and benefit from them doesn't require you to be a scholar or a mystic, or even to have a lot of prior experience with Buddhism. Anyone who has the time and interest to study those great teachings can reap profound rewards—particularly if you have a little guidance, and if you then bring those teachings with you onto the meditation cushion.

The inspiration for this book first came from the series of brilliant Dharma talks Reb Anderson Roshi gave on the *Sutra of the Explanation of the Profound Secrets* (*Samdhinirmocana Sutra*). There are so many sutras and so many confusing and seemingly contradictory teachings that it is easy to be overwhelmed, but in those talks Reb spelled out in simple, contemporary language the way the teachings of the three turnings of the wheel, outlined in that sutra, can help us make sense of it all. So I set out to write a book that told the great story of the three turnings of the wheel in a way that would draw in contemporary readers, no matter what their background, and make the connection of those teachings to meditation practice clear. I have quoted extensively from key passages in the sutras and then tried to explain them from a straightforward, twenty-first-century perspective that anyone can understand. Even though I highly recommend it, it isn't necessary to go back to read translations of the original texts to see the full scope of this great story unfold. All that is required is your sincerity and an open mind. It is my deepest hope that this book will provide some of the same kind of encouragement and guidance that Reb's talks gave to me.

This book is the result of the labors of innumerable people, and it is only possible thank a few. First off, I want express my deepest appreciation and gratitude to all my teachers, especially Reb Anderson Roshi, Toni Packer, Lama Palden Drolma, and Rose Taylor Goldfield, as well as to my wife Claudia Royal Coleman. In addition to Reb and Claudia, Lois Richerson, Jason Siff, Coleen LeDrew Elgin, Hugh Platt, and Rosemary Donnell read early drafts of the manuscript and were of enormous help. My gratitude also goes out to the people at Wisdom Publication and especially Laura Cunningham, whose careful editing and insightful comments made this a far better book, Josh Bartok for believing in this project, and Ben Gleason, Lindsay D'Andrea, and Lydia Anderson. It is great to work with people who really understand Buddhism. Finally, I want to thank all those I have practiced with over the years who have shown such a sincere commitment to study and practice the Dharma. Without your inspiration I never would have undertaken this project.

Introduction: The Wheel of Dharma

We live our lives in a dream. A dream so vivid and compelling that few of us ever realize that it is nothing but a figment of the imagination, no more real than a desert mirage or a flower made of clouds in the sky. We tell ourselves endless stories imagining our lives as some great drama with us in the staring role. Every new twist and turn keeps us riveted to the story and the cauldron of our emotions on boil. Of course, at some level we know that we are not really the center of the universe, but our dreams are far too powerful for that to make much difference. We may have moments when the clouds part and we experience the pristine clarity of our own true nature, but it is seldom long before our old habits of dullness, greed, and fear drag us back to those mesmerizing delusions.

Since a buddha is always awake, you might think that she never dreams. But to be truly awake is to feel boundless compassion for those still suffering in the world of delusion, and that compassion leads the buddhas back into our dream of separation and suffering—over and over again—back to show us a different dream. Make no mistake about it: even the words of a buddha are part of our web of concepts, ideas, stories, and dreams. But a buddha's dream is a wholesome dream: a dream of peace, a dream of love, a dream of liberation—a dream that shows us how to wake up from our dreams.

Turning the Wheel of Dharma

The great wheel of Buddhist teachings has been spinning for more than two thousand years, and it has left a vast ocean of Dharma. A hundred generations of continuous practice, teaching, and reflection have left us with more treasures of wisdom than anyone can even count, let alone read and assimilate. Fortunately, there is no reason we have to. In a very real sense, the teachings simply say the same thing over and over again in endless new languages to an ever-changing audience. At the heart of all true Dharma there is a timeless wisdom beyond language or conception, and the wheel of the teachings spins round and round it, pointing the way back to its source.

Despite its jawbreaking name, the great *Samdhinirmocana Sutra* (pronounced "samde nir mo chana"), or *Sutra of the Explanation of the Profound Secrets*, can do a lot to help us make sense of all those teachings and to see how they fit together. It tells us of three "turnings of this wheel of Dharma," each with its own distinctive teachings building upon, but not replacing, its predecessors.

In the first turning of the wheel, the Buddha, like a doctor diagnosing a disease, spelled out the cause of suffering and what to do about it in clear unambiguous terms; these are called the "four noble truths." The first of the noble truths he taught is that the unenlightened life is full of suffering. Second, he identified the cause of suffering: craving and attachment. Third, he made it clear that craving and attachment can be ended, and in the fourth noble truth he laid out his treatment program— the noble eightfold path. He told his followers that if they behaved with ethics and compassion, meditated diligently, and cultivated wisdom based on his teachings, they could end their suffering and achieve the ultimate release of nirvana. In these teachings, suffering is the disease; craving is the cause; the eightfold path of wisdom, ethical conduct, and meditation is the cure; and freedom is the result.

Even though the Buddha often warned his followers not to make his teachings into just something else to cling to, many people found them so profound and helpful that they did exactly that. So in the second turning, the Buddha did something unprecedented in the history of world religion. He dropped a bombshell that blew apart that clinging and along with it everything else many of the followers of his earliest teachings believed. In the *Diamond Sutra* the Buddha tells us that he really has nothing at all to teach and that anyone who says he does slanders him. In the *Heart Sutra*, we are told that everything, absolutely everything, is empty. And in that emptiness, there is no suffering, no cause of suffering, no end of suffering, and no noble path to lead from suffering. The Buddha seemed to be denying all his own teachings!

Obviously, the radical wisdom of the second turning is, as the sutras often say, "difficult, extremely difficult to understand," and it left a lot of people amazed and confused. The sutras even tell us that when some of the Buddha's followers first heard those teachings they fell down, vomited blood, and died. Inevitably, some mistook those new teachings for some kind of shocking rejection of the older ones, while others fell victim to a kind of nihilism, reasoning that if everything is empty then nothing really matters and they are free to do whatever they please regardless of the consequences for others.

The third turning of the wheel sought to rectify such mistaken beliefs and provide more guidance to those who seemed to have had their feet cut out from under them. The first step was to explain the apparent contradictions between the first turning of the wheel and the second. In the *Sutra of the Explanation of the Profound Secrets* the Buddha tells us that words are just "conventional designations" that he uses to help free us from suffering, and that no matter how different they seem, all the teachings are of "one taste." Like a good doctor, the Buddha gave different medicines to different patients depending on their individual needs. He might tell one person about the four noble truths, and in his next breath tell someone else that those truths were completely empty, but the goal was always the same—to free them from their suffering.

The teachings of the third turning go on to give more explicit guidance to practitioners by painting a profound picture of the way the conscious and subconscious minds operate, and of the inconceivable ultimate—the awakened buddha nature—from which they arise.

Some people may take these teachings as nothing more than abstract philosophy that doesn't make much difference in the real world, but the Buddha never really cared much about philosophy. He cared about freeing people from their suffering, and these teachings can do exactly that. Their wisdom not only provides the key to free us from our endless chains of deluded thought but also serves as a practical guide to lead practitioners to progressively deeper stages of meditation. Following the teachings of the first turning, we learn to purify and refine our behavior, release our cravings, and ultimately to see the emptiness of self. In the second turning, we go even deeper to realize not just the emptiness of self, but the emptiness of absolutely everything else as well. Finally, the teachings of the third turning point us directly to the ultimate at the source of all appearance and all emptiness—to our awakened buddha nature beyond all description or understanding.

Now that the Buddhist teachings are coming to the West, they are once again being retold and reshaped to meet a new cultural context. But in confronting the postmodern world, Buddhism must adopt to a more radical change in cultural and economic circumstances than at any other time in its more than two thousand years of history. Old doctrines are being put in new words, and while some resonate with their new audience, others fall on deaf ears and are being downplayed or abandoned. With the notable exception of quantum physics, which resonates most strongly with the teachings of the second turning,[1] it is striking how much these new influences and approaches, from modern psychology and "brain science" to secular mindfulness training, share with the approach of the first turning. These teachings identify a problem, make a rational systematic analysis of its causes, and propose a method to cure it. They have a clear-cut goal that one can achieve by making a diligent effort to apply the proper remedies.

Our challenge now is to integrate the great wisdom of the other two turnings into our emerging understanding of the Buddhist path and apply that understanding to the new world we inhabit. Just as the teachings of the second turning cut the ground out from under those who clung to the certainty and the status offered by their understanding of the Buddha's original teachings, the same lesson needs to be learned on a much broader scale, whether it concerns religious beliefs, political and social ideologies, or even the science that seems to offer us an objective view of the world. Like the Buddha's teachings themselves, Western science offers amazingly useful and profound ideas, but we often forget that they are still just ideas. In the last analysis, the wondrous mystery of the world remains beyond our conceptual grasp, and we forget this at great risk to ourselves and our world. Again and again, history has shown us that when we come to accept any system of ideas, no matter how useful or profound, as absolute truth, conflict and division are the inevitable result.

But it is not enough to realize the emptiness of scientific knowledge or of the political and social ideologies that guide our lives, or even to realize the inconceivable nature of reality. Our concepts and ideas may be empty, but we still need them to relate to each other and to function in the world. Many people in the West are becoming familiar with the great emptiness teachings of the second turning, but by themselves they can leave us rudderless, or even worse, we may come to believe that since all ideas and beliefs are empty, the rules of ethical behavior no longer apply. The teachings of the third turning are less well known, but they are vitally important because they can guide us to the middle way between believing in the dreams we weave and the nihilism that can arise if we lose our bearings in the great sea of emptiness.

Before we move on, a point of confusion needs to be cleared up. Buddhists love putting their beliefs into numbered lists, and another three-part classification—the three vehicles (*yanas* in Sanskrit)—can easily be confused with the three turnings of the wheel. In this other scheme, the first yana is the Hinayana (literally, the lesser vehicle)—a pejorative term that was given to the earliest Buddhist schools by their Mahayana competitors. Since the Theravada tradition of Sri Lanka and Southeast Asia is the only one of these early schools that is still in practice, it is common these days to substitute "Theravada" for "Hinayana" to avoid any kind of judgment about the value of these different traditions. The Mahayana, or "great vehicle," which is most firmly established in East Asia, came next; and the last to develop was the Vajrayana, or "diamond vehicle," which is most influential in Tibet and the surrounding Himalayan regions. A few teachers and scholars use the three turnings of the wheel and the three yanas interchangeably, but it is better to keep them separate so that the three turnings refer solely to Buddhist teachings, while the three yanas describe much broader traditions that include rituals, practices, and styles of organization. This is important because while the Theravadan school relies more or less exclusively on the teachings of the first turning, the teachings of all three turnings are accepted in both Mahayana and Vajrayana Buddhism.

The Foundations of This Book

If you gaze out over this vast ocean of Dharma, it is easy to feel a bit seasick. So many great teachers have given so many great teachings, it seems no one could even have read, much less, understood them all. I certainly haven't. Rather, what I have tried to do as best I can is mine the seabed of that great ocean of Buddhist wisdom for the ore from which to forge a new postmodern understanding that is tempered by the modern scientific and social thought of our day.

My strategy in trying to plumb so vast a field is to rely, insofar as possible, on the classic texts of the Buddhist tradition usually known by their Sanskrit name of "sutras." In the Theravadan tradition, which relies on the Pali language, they are called "suttas," but since the teachings of all three turnings were recorded in Sanskrit, but only the teachings of the first turning come down to us in Pali, we will use the Sanskrit term for them all.[2] These sutras (or suttas if you prefer) are held to be the direct words of the Buddha or a high-level bodhisattva, and as such they hold a very special place in the Buddhist tradition. Through the centuries, there have also been a huge number of commentaries on the sutras written in India, Sri Lanka, China, Japan, Korea, Southeast Asia, Tibet, and now even in the West. While many of them are extremely highly regarded in one tradition, they are often unknown, ignored, or even rejected in another. The sutras, on the other hand, are far more likely to be read, practiced, and revered in multiple traditions, and so they provide a firmer foundation for a Buddhist understanding that cuts across Asia's sectarian divides.

Of course, many scholars doubt that the historical Buddha was the real source of some or even all of the sutras. The oldest group of sutras, often known as the Pali Canon because they come down to us from the Theravadan tradition in the Pali language, are the ones scholars consider most likely to be the words of the first historical Buddha. But written language wasn't in common use in the India of the Buddha's time, and those teachings were not put to writing until some three hundred years after his death. Until then, they were the subject of one of the most prodigious feats of rote memory in human history. Generations of monks memorized, double-checked, and passed along the Buddha's talks and teachings, which, when finally put into writing, ran to thousands of pages. But the Buddha never saw or approved those texts, so it is possible that some of them were based more on the views of the monks who claim to have heard them than the Buddha's actual words, or that they were subject to systematic biases that came from the monks' failure to understand their deepest meaning.

But what of the Mahayana sutras that do not appear in the early Buddhist canon and were not written down until even later? One obvious possibility is that some of them were also teachings of the original Buddha that were also passed along by memory, but for one reason or another were excluded from the orthodox canon when the monks assembled to decide what was to be included and what was not. They may also be the words of some later buddha or buddhas, for in the Buddhist tradition everyone has the potential to become a buddha and countless beings actually have. Or on the other hand, some of them may have been the product of advanced meditation masters who went into a deep trance visualizing a buddha or a great bodhisattva and asked them questions about the Dharma. But even if there were some way to know for sure, for our purposes it doesn't really matter where the great sutras of the three turnings came from. What matters is the wisdom they contain.

There is, however, another problem. There are thousands of pages in the Pali Canon alone, and thousands more Mahayana sutras survive that vary in length from just a single letter to over fifteen hundred pages, so the question of which of these sources to rely on is a big one. Fortunately, over the centuries of study and practice a few sutras have come to stand out either as being especially deep and profound or as a classic representations of an important school of thought, and it is on those we will rely.

Analytically brilliant, complex, and psychologically penetrating, the *Sutra of the Explanation of the Profound Secrets* is the rock on which this book is built. I have read and reread the three English translations of this sutra for over a decade,[3] listened to Reb Anderson Roshi's brilliant commentaries on the sutra, and eventually helped him to edit them into a book published in 2012 as *The Third Turning of the Wheel*. That process changed my life, and I became convinced that the wisdom of this sutra needed to be more widely known in the West. If you have never heard of the *Sutra of the Explanation of the Profound Secrets*, you are hardly alone, but it is the source of the great school of Mahayana Buddhist philosophy known as the Yogacara, and it was probably the first sutra to tell us that the Buddha's teachings could be divided into three separate turnings of the wheel.

The *Lion's Roar of Queen Srimala* and the *Lankavatara Sutra* will help us fill in the teachings of the third turning that aren't in the *Sutra of the Explanation of the Profound Secrets*. These two are considered *tathagatagarbha* sutras (a term that literally means "the womb or embryo of the Buddha"), since they helped introduce the idea that there is an awakened buddha nature that lies within us all. Finally, there is the *Avatamsaka Sutra,* or *Flower Ornament Sutra*, which runs to over fifteen hundred pages in its English translation and in some respects puts the finishing touches on the great edifice of classic Buddhist philosophy.

Just as the *Sutra of the Explanation of the Profound Secrets* began the third turning of the wheel, its great predecessor, the *Diamond Sutra,* is the most likely candidate for the credit of setting the second turning of the wheel of Dharma in motion, and we will examine it closely.[4] The *Heart Sutra* is the best known of all the sutras of the second turning, and it will also receive our close attention. It is a masterpiece of concise expression—it can be written on a single page, yet it expresses the heart of the vast body of literature that brought the elusive concept of *shunyata* (emptiness) to the forefront of Buddhist practice and belief.

Our foundation for the exploration of the teachings of the first turning will be the *Dhammacakkappavattana Sutta*, or the *Sutra on Setting in Motion the Wheel of Dharma*, from the Pali Canon. It records the historical Buddha's first discourse and provides a wonderful summary of the wisdom of the first turning as well as a handy framework to integrate the teachings from other great sutras we'll investigate, such as the *Kandaraka Sutta* and the *Satipatthana Sutta* (*Sutra on the Foundations of Mindfulness*).[5]

The wisdom of these sutras is universal and timeless, but our personal understanding, at least until we are fully awakened, is always limited by our culture and experience. We have to do more than just translate these great teachings into our language; we have to bring them to life in our own cultural terms—and that is the goal of the second part of this book. Chapter 4 attempts to summarize the great psychological teachings of the sutras in a way that resonates with our own cultural perspectives, and outlines the way the sutras can guide us in putting their understanding into practice. For most of us, however, just reading and studying the sutras on our own is not enough; we need the guidance and support of a wise teacher. So the next two chapters show us how two great meditation masters bring these teachings to life. Chapter 5 comes from one of the most influential Zen teachers in the West, Reb Anderson Roshi, and chapter 6 is by one of our leading Vajrayana teachers, Lama Palden Drolma. Together they not only give us an idea how invaluable the guidance and support of a good teacher can be, but they also provide some insight into the different approaches of their two traditions.

Finally, I have a piece of advice to offer those who are about to embark on this journey into the wisdom of the great sutras. Our relentlessly competitive educational system leaves a lot of us with a deep feeling of inadequacy. A few students are held up as stars, while most of the rest of us are left to feel that somehow we just don't cut it. So when we come upon something that we have trouble understanding, we may feel those old anxieties and be tempted to just give up and turn away. But understanding the wisdom of the great sutras has nothing to do with being an "A" student. Anyone can do it. All you need is the faith to believe that the wisdom of those sutras can indeed transform your life, and the willingness to keep at it and let the teachings unfold in their own time. As you progress along this path, you are bound to encounter some teachings that you just don't understand—especially when you study the profound and mysterious wisdom of the second turning. When you come upon teachings like that, just reflect on them for a while and move on. If you go back and revisit them from time to time, eventually they will open themselves to you.

On the other hand, be very careful when you think you grasp some new teaching the first time you encounter it. These great teachings contain layers upon layers of meaning, and too much confidence in a shallow understanding is a barrier to any further growth. My advice is just to dive into the sea of Dharma and keep on swimming. Sooner or later you are bound to reach the other shore.

Part I

The Three Turnings
of the Wheel

The First Turning of the Wheel:
Freedom and the Four Noble Truths

The Buddha didn't write a holy book that claimed to be beyond all cultural or historical interpretation. His teachings arose spontaneously out of his interactions with the different people he encountered, so in a very real sense, his questioners were as much a part of the teachings as the Buddha himself. The Pali Canon shows us that he gave very different teachings to different kinds of people. He even gave different answers to the same questions depending on who was asking and what would be most helpful to them at the time. To laypeople, he would emphasize generosity and ethical behavior, to monks his focus was on renunciation and meditation practice. He gave a teaching known as the Fire Sermon to a group of Hindus who worshiped Agni, the god of fire, and meditation instructions to a musician by comparing it to the tuning of a lute. So to understand the teachings of the first turning, we need to understand their social context.

The Buddha's India

The Buddha's teachings were part of a worldwide transformation in human thought so sweeping and profound that it has been called the Axial Age. Although no one is really sure why it happened, between the eighth and third centuries BCE the human world turned on its axis and took a new direction. Although as far as we know there was no direct contact between them, great sages such as Confucius and Lao Tzu in China and Socrates, Plato, and Aristotle in Greece were leading transformations in their own lands, just as the Buddha and other great Indian thinkers were in theirs. Until this Axial Age, religion and for that matter almost all human understanding had been based on myths and stories. The stories of spirits, gods, and great ancestors were told and retold through the generations, celebrated in song and dance, and recreated in rituals, and they provided the warp and weave of human culture.

Perhaps it was because this was a time of rapid social change, or that all these lands were ruled by competing states beset by fierce internal and external conflicts, or perhaps it was just the growing maturity of human culture, but whatever the reason, some great thinkers began stepping back from their myths and stories and took a critical look at the world.[6] They developed the first philosophic systems to present a cohesive rational explanation of the world. Unlike their tribal predecessors, they created universalistic ethical systems that demanded justice and fair treatment for those outside their own group. And even more radically, they took a critical view of everyday life and of the larger social world. They described the sources of human suffering and gave us new ideals of how to think and behave. They even took on established social power, creating far-reaching new ideals about what makes a good society and how it should be run, and then judging their rulers on how well they lived up to them.

The Buddha was born in India in one of the most wondrous eras of human history, every bit the equal of ancient Greece, classic China, or Renaissance Italy. But it was a world so different from our own that it is easy to misunderstand. By modern standards it was slow paced and traditional. People lived by farming or tending herds of animals, and life was dominated by the rhythms of the seasons, the demands of the earth, and the constraints of tradition. Most people lived their whole lives in the confines of the small village where they grew up, seldom wandering more than a few miles from their home. They knew virtually every person they met during the day, and communication with the outside world was rare. In comparison to us, their technology was certainly primitive, but the land was rich and the population low so most people probably enjoyed a fairly comfortable life.

But that doesn't mean social life was egalitarian. In many parts of India, religion and culture were dominated by a class of hereditary priests who saw society as a rigid hierarchy with themselves at the top. These Brahmans carried on elaborate and expensive rituals that completely excluded the common people. If the Brahmans failed to perform these rituals correctly, the very survival of society and all human life was believed to be threatened. Politically, the power rested in the hands of another hereditary class—the warrior nobility. In some places, like the tribal republic in which the Buddha was born, their leader was a hereditary prince, but in others he was chosen by a council of tribal leaders.

But the Buddha lived in a time of sweeping change, and the growth of a new social order was threatening this closed, traditional world. Aggressive new empires spread across India, bringing sweeping changes with them. Many parts of India were seeing a rapid expansion of trade and commerce as the use of money grew. While most people continued to live in rural villages, new cities sprang up, spreading a new cosmopolitanism. As the power of the royalty and the flourishing merchant classes grew, they became increasingly discontent with the cultural domination of the Brahmans, with all their costly rituals and claims of social superiority, and there was a creative explosion of new ideas about the world and our place in it.

The Indians are among the greatest religious philosophers the world has ever known, but they haven't shown the same interest in history, and much about their past remains obscure. Most of what we know about the Buddha's life comes from the records of his own talks, and there is little independent verification. He was probably born a prince or nobleman in one of the tribal republics of northern India on the periphery of the sphere of Brahmanical influence. It is traditionally held that he renounced his life of privilege and left home at the age of twenty-nine to become one of the wandering philosophers and religious seekers of India's Axial Age known as *sramanas* or "strivers."

These holy men (women were generally excluded) were highly respected, and people were usually willing to give them enough food so they didn't have to work. This freedom allowed an amazing explosion of religious creativity among competing teachers, even if they shared little except a distrust of the old religion of priestly rituals. Some teachers advocated austerities and self-mortification, others sensualism and self-indulgence; some were materialists who believed life ended at death and that was it, while many others felt that life and death were linked together in a long chain of birth and rebirth. In addition to the Buddha, the founders of Jainism and modern Hinduism are also to be counted among them.

The Middle Way

The Buddha lived for some forty years after his great enlightenment and devoted them all to teaching the Dharma, so he left us an abundance of teachings. Fortunately, the sutras contain many good summaries of his key teachings, and among the best is the *The Sutra on Setting in Motion the Wheel of Dharma*. It provides a concise introduction to the teachings of the first turning, and it will be our point of departure.

This sutra describes the first teachings the Buddha gave after his great enlightenment, thus setting "the wheel of Dharma in motion." It was addressed to the five men (he calls them *bhikkhus*, or "monks") who had originally been his followers but who left when he decided that starving himself, and practicing other extreme austerities so common among the sramanas, wasn't the right path to enlightenment. The Buddha begins right off telling them of the fallacy of that approach:

> Bhikkhus, these two extremes should not be followed by one who has gone forth into homelessness. What two? The pursuit of sensual happiness in sensual pleasures, which is low, vulgar, the way of worldlings, ignoble, unbeneficial; and the pursuit of self-mortification, which is painful, ignoble, unbeneficial. Without veering toward either of these extremes, the Tathagata has awakened to the middle way, which gives rise to vision, which gives rise to knowledge, which leads to peace, to direct knowledge, to enlightenment, to nibbana.[7]

"Tathagata" is the term the Buddha often used to refer to himself, and "nibbana" is the Pali word for "nirvana." Thus, the Buddha is saying that his great doctrine of "the middle way," which rejects the extremes of both sensualism and self-mortification so popular among the seekers of his day, is the way to reach enlightenment—a balanced life is necessary to follow the spiritual path to its goal.

Although the Buddha taught many householders and did not insist that all of his followers become monks, he clearly saw renunciation as the path to awakening. He himself remained a celibate renunciate for all the decades after his enlightenment and never returned to family life. Thus, it is not surprising that he begins by condemning the pursuit of sensual pleasure so typical of everyday life. But then, he turns to also reject the austerities and self-mortification that were held in such high esteem by his first followers and so many of their fellow spiritual seekers. The Buddha told his monks that they must give up their families, avoid all sexual contact, and live a life of the utmost simplicity, yet they must also take care of their physical health and the needs of their bodies. Over the years, this doctrine of the middle way came to be applied to more philosophical issues as well, rejecting those who cling one-sidedly to one philosophical extreme or another.

Next, the Buddha describes what it means to follow this middle way in more detail:

> And what, bhikkhus, is that middle way awakened to by the Tathagata, which gives rise to vision . . . which leads to Nibbana? It is this Noble Eightfold Path; that is, right view, right intention, right speech, right action, right livelihood, right effort, right mindfulness, right concentration. This is that middle way awakened to by the Tathagata, which gives rise to vision, which gives rise to knowledge, which leads to peace, to direct knowledge, to enlightenment, to Nibbana.[8]

This is the famous noble eightfold path that provides step-by-step instructions for liberating oneself from suffering and reaching nirvana.

The Four Noble Truths

After this brief presentation, the Buddha goes on to describe the second of his most famous doctrines: the four noble truths. The eightfold path and the four truths are not, however, really separate. The fourth noble truth is the eightfold path, and the first factor in the eightfold path, right view, is in part the wisdom based on an understanding of the four noble truths. So they form an interlocking circle.

The *Sutra on Setting in Motion the Wheel of Dharma* gives this description of the first noble truth, known as the truth of suffering:

> Now this, bhikkhus, is the noble truth of suffering: birth is suffer-
> ing, aging is suffering, illness is suffering, death is suffering; union
> with what is displeasing is suffering; separation from what is pleas-
> ing is suffering; not to get what one wants is suffering; in brief, the
> five aggregates subject to clinging are suffering.[9]

The truth of suffering is deep and profound, but perhaps not surprisingly, it is often misunderstood. Because the Buddha, alone among the world's great religious thinkers, focused on the problem of suffering and what to do about it with a laser-like intensity, Buddhism is often viewed as a negative religion that sees life as nothing more than misery. But that is not what the first noble truth says. The teachings of the first turning often recognize, for example, the joy that comes from compassionate unselfish behavior.

Rather than understanding the first noble truth as "life *is* suffering," it would be better to say, "life *has* suffering"—something even the harshest critics of Buddhism would not deny. But even that statement may be too strong, for the word translated as "suffering," *dukkha*, doesn't mean exactly the same thing in Sanskrit or Pali as it does in English. Many scholars consider "unsatisfactoriness" a more accurate translation, because dukkha is a much broader term than suffering. The overwhelming suffering of losing one's child is dukkha, but so is the discomfort when you run out of coffee and you have to wait three hours for your first cup.

This unsatisfactoriness nonetheless pervades all aspects of life, for as the Buddha put it, "separation from what is pleasing is suffering." Even life's most joyous and happy moments can cause us suffering, simply because they are impermanent and subject to constant change. But loss isn't the only source of our suffering. We desire many things we don't have, and this makes us suffer too, because "not to get what one wants is suffering." Yet even if there was some perfect world where we had everything we wanted, the Buddha tells us that we would still suffer, because "union with what is displeasing is suffering." The Buddha repeatedly mentions four of the most obvious examples: birth, old age, sickness, and death, but the list could go on and on. Everyday life, then, is unsatisfactory and full of difficulty.

The second noble truth is called the truth of the cause of suffering:

> Now this, bhikkhus, is the noble truth of the origin of suffering: it is this craving which leads to renewed existence, accompanied by delight and lust, seeking delight here and there; that is, craving for sensual pleasures, craving for existence, craving for extermination.[10]

Most of the time when we feel bad, we blame it on the world: I'm miserable because my husband left me, my children don't respect me, or I lost my job. The Buddha advocates a radically different view, saying that our suffering isn't caused by anything in the outside world; it's caused by our own craving.

Our suffering comes from our desire for sensual pleasure: good food, great sex, and a comfortable bed. Our suffering also comes from our "craving for existence"; we want to be better looking, smarter, healthier, and more powerful. This craving for achievement, to become something better, lies at the very heart of our competitive individualistic culture, but we can also interpret the craving for existence to be the craving simply for more life and more experiences. But the craving for sensual pleasure or new experiences isn't the only thing that causes our suffering. Sometimes it is all too much, and we crave extinction: extinction of our pain, our confusion, our hopelessness, and sometimes even our lives. So craving is the key; our suffering does not come from sensual indulgence or even our physical and emotional pain. It comes from our inability to accept things as they are. We suffer because we cling to what we like and push away what we don't.

This is what the Buddha means when he said, "the five aggregates subject to clinging are suffering." In the teachings of the first turning, all human experience was seen to be made up of a rapid succession of momentary individual events. These "dharmas" (with a small "d") came to be seen as the basic building blocks of the world and of personal experience, something similar to the way the atoms postulated by today's physicists are believed to make up matter. The dharmas were classified together into five separate "heaps" or aggregates: forms, feelings, perceptions, mental formations, and consciousness. Although this brief sutra doesn't mention it, this is where the famous doctrine of *anatman* or "no self" comes in.

Although our experience is nothing but a cavalcade of fleeting momentary events, we take ourselves to be discrete autonomous individuals. In other words, we mistakenly believe that there is some kind of "me" or "self" that experiences these dharmas and provides coherence and an underlying unity, and that those heaps of experiences make up some kind of independent "me." Although that in itself might not be much of a problem, what inevitably happens is that we cling to those aggregates and to the self we imagine to be experiencing them. We cling to what we perceive as "I," "me," and "mine." We try to preserve, protect, and promote that imagined self, and then we suffer.

Given this analysis of the problem of suffering, the solution is obvious, and the Buddha goes on to state it in the third noble truth:

> Now this, bhikkhus, is the noble truth of the cessation of suffering: the remainderless fading away and cessation of that same craving, the giving up and relinquishing of it, freedom from it, nonreliance on it.[11]

The essence of the Buddha's message is not that life has suffering— that was hardly news—but that there can be an end to suffering. If we end our craving, completely, totally, and without remainder, we end our suffering—in other words, we reach nirvana. According the Buddha's *Mahasunnata Sutta*, or *Greater Discourse on Emptiness*, "When he [a monk] abides contemplating rise and fall in these five aggregates affected by clinging, the conceit 'I am' based on these five aggregates affected by clinging is abandoned in him."[12] In other words, when the monk observes how temporary the aggregates are, he abandons the belief he has some kind of a separate individual self. And when we abandon our notion of a separate self, we can abandon our cravings—after all, if there is no "I," how can "I" want anything?—and we can abandon suffering itself and enter nirvana.

Most people know that the Buddha held nirvana to be the most exalted of all states and the highest possible happiness, but what exactly is it? As is typical in the teachings of the first turning, nirvana is explained mainly by telling us what it isn't. As a result, some Westerners think the Buddha advocated some kind of metaphysical nihilism, but actually, he repeatedly condemned all nihilistic views and held that nirvana was the ultimate state of complete peace and the culmination of the path. The problem is that nirvana can really only be understood by experiencing it; words can best tell us what it isn't, not what it is.

Nirvana literally means something like "blowing out," "cooling down," "unbinding" or "extinguishing." In the *Nibbana Sutta*, nirvana is described as "unborn—unbecome—unmade—unfabricated."[13] In Sanskrit, the word is formed by the negative term "nir" combined with the root which means "to blow." So the reference is to blowing out a flame—the flame of craving and attachment.

The last of the noble truths is the path that leads from suffering to liberation:

> Now this, monks, is the noble truth of the way leading to the cessation of suffering: it is this Noble Eightfold Path; that is, right view, right intention, right speech, right action, right livelihood, right effort, right mindfulness, right concentration.[14]

So the final noble truth closes the circle and brings in the Buddha's other most famous set of teachings.

The Eightfold Path

Although there is clearly a logic in the ordering of the eight steps on the path, they are not really progressive in the sense that you complete the first one, then move on to the next and the next until you are done. They are more like intertwining strands of a single rope that requires the contributions of all the other strands for maximum strength. So it might be better to call them factors rather than steps.

Countless practitioners and scholars have studied and restudied the eightfold path over the years, and many have found it useful to divide those eight steps into three groups: wisdom, ethical conduct, and meditation. The factors of wisdom—right view and right intention—come first, because they provide the fundamental orientation for all the others, but at the same time their perfection is also the ultimate fruit of the path. Next come the instructions on how followers of the path should lead their lives (ethical conduct), and finally there are the teachings on the meditation practices that lead to the fruition of wisdom and thus back to the first steps on the path.

Right view can also be translated as right outlook or right understanding. It is simply the right way to look at the world in order to see it as it really is. One of the most basic truths to see is the reality of karma (or *kamma*, in Pali).

As the Buddha put it in a different sutra:

> Beings are the owners of their kamma, the heirs of their kamma; they have kamma as their origin, kamma as their relative, kamma as their resort; whatever kamma they do, good or bad, they are its heirs.[15]

Thus, the law of karma is a simple one: act from positive intentions and the results either in this life or the next will be good ones, but if your intentions are selfish or cruel the result will be more suffering. This understanding, in turn, becomes the foundation for the factors involving ethical conduct: right speech, right action, right livelihood.

Another part of right view is the understanding of the four noble truths we just examined—that suffering is one of the basic marks of existence, that it's caused by craving, that freedom from craving is possible, and that the way to release craving is by following the noble eightfold path. Right view also recognizes that the world is marked by two other basic characteristics, in addition to suffering: impermanence and the absence of self. The idea that everything is impermanent and subject to change is hardly a controversial one. Although most of us don't like to think about it, we all know we are going to die, and science tells us that the great mountains and rivers, even the sun itself, will all eventually pass away. The truth of the absence of self is harder to prove empirically, but in deep meditation the realization gradually dawns on us that all our ideas and beliefs about ourselves and the images we have of what we are, are nothing more than that— just ideas, images, and beliefs. Search as we may, we can never find the entity to which we think they refer. At first, the understanding of these profound truths is likely to merely be intellectual. But as we practice the other factors of the path, we experience the reality to which these words refer more and more deeply until they finally culminate in liberation itself.

Right intention, which is sometimes translated as right resolve, is the aspiration to follow the path and live according to right view. There are, however, countless levels and refinements of right intention. Many people start by resolving to be more kind and compassionate, others resolve to live their lives more mindfully, and still others may even take monastic vows and completely renounce the worldly life.

After the two factors of wisdom come the three factors of ethical conduct: right speech, right action, and right livelihood. The subject of Buddhist ethics is a vast one, and other sutras and commentaries treat it in great detail, but their essence is captured in this short verse from the *Dhammapada*: "To abstain from all evil, to cultivate the good, and to purify one's mind—this is the teaching of the Buddha."[16]

The first component of ethical conduct is "right speech," and the Buddha sets a high standard that is often hard for even the most dedicated practitioners to follow. We should, he tells us, never say things that are not true. Nor should we say things intended to harm another even if they are true. Our speech should never be harsh, but always loving and kind. And most difficult of all for many of us, we must not engage in idle chatter, but only say that which needs to be said. The wise person, in the Buddha's view, maintains a noble silence until the time is right to speak.

The next ethical factor, right action, can of course be displayed in an infinite variety of ways, but the Buddha did lay down some guidelines. At a minimum, lay Buddhists are expected to follow five basic precepts of ethical conduct: to refrain from harming living beings, stealing, sexual misconduct, harmful speech, and intoxication. Westerners tend to look at these precepts as absolute rules, something like the Ten Commandments. But as the influential contemporary Buddhist Thich Nhat Hanh puts it, they are more like signposts pointing the way to a better life than laws or unbreakable prohibitions.[17] Following these precepts is not a goal in itself, but a way to help calm the mind, accumulate merit, and speed the practitioner's progress along the path to liberation. The goal is enlightenment. Ethical conduct is critically important, but only as a means to help us get to that goal. To drive this point home, Thich Nhat Hanh doesn't even call them precepts, but rather "mindfulness trainings."[18]

A fully enlightened being exhibits a spontaneous morality that transcends any specific set of rules or precepts. But until that state is reached, the precepts are an essential guide along the way, not only for the average person, but for those who have some real degree of realization as well. All too often, even great teachers have fallen victim to the adulation of their followers and let an inflated view of themselves lead them to believe they are no longer bound by the need to follow the precepts. A fully realized being may not need ethical guidelines, but for anyone who still has unexplored reservoirs of greed, hate, and delusion, the almost inevitable result of abandoning the precepts too soon will be self-serving and abusive behavior.

The first of the precepts is clear enough: do not kill. What that means in practice is, however, a complex issue, since one literally cannot live without at least inadvertently taking life. The general idea is to avoid all violent thoughts and actions unless there is no other possible option. Vegetarianism, for example, was often recommended as being less harmful to other forms of life than eating meat, but no one was expected to give up meat if that was the only healthy food available.

The second admonition is "do not take what is not given," which simply means do not steal, and perhaps more broadly, do not to take anything that isn't freely offered. Down through the centuries, the Buddhist ideal has always been a simple life that takes as little as possible from the land and shares as much as possible with others.

The third precept is more complex: abstain from sexual misconduct. The Buddha did give some specific guidelines: a man (the Buddha never discussed the issue from a woman's point of view, although similar prohibitions were later applied to them) may not have sex with anyone still under the protection of their relatives, nor with married women, female convicts, or betrothed girls. These rules have, however, been interpreted flexibly. As Buddhism spread out from India, it usually just adopted the cultural standards of its new home. But the underlying principle was always the same: avoid any sexual behavior that is harmful to oneself, one's partners, or the community at large.

The fourth precept is the abstaining from lying and harmful speech, and the Buddha considered it so important he made right speech one of the steps in the eightfold path, as we discussed above.

Finally, the Buddha advised his lay followers not to become intoxicated to the point where they might violate the other precepts. Some take this to be a total prohibition on the consumption of any alcohol or drugs, but the more common interpretation is not to use them to the point of heedlessness.

The Buddha had far higher expectations for his monks than for his lay followers. He required them to take on hundreds of additional precepts including complete celibacy, never touching money, and not eating after noon. Westerners are sometime shocked at how restrictive those monastic precepts are, but following these strict precepts was never seen as an end in itself, but a way to clarify and focus the mind.

The last ethical factor, right livelihood, could obviously be seen as a subcategory of right action, but the Buddha apparently felt it was so important that it also deserved specific mention. Like sexual misconduct, what is considered right livelihood in one time and place may not be the same in another, but the general principles are clear. One should make a living in a way that is peaceful and beneficial to the world, and one should not be involved in deception, coercion, violence, or any actions that would encourage others to break the precepts.

The last three factors concern meditation—right effort, right mindfulness, and right concentration. All the factors on the path work to support each other, and that is certainly true of these three. The great Western translator and commentator Bhikkhu Bodhi illustrates the point with a short story:[19] Three boys go to the park to play, and they see some lovely flowers at the top of a tree. Even the tallest boy can't reach them, so one boy bends over and offers to let the tallest boy stand on his back. But the tall boy's perch is too wobbly for him to stand still, so the third boy comes over and offers his shoulder to steady him. The tallest boy, standing on the back of the second boy and leaning on the shoulder of the third boy, reaches up and gathers their prize. In this story, the boy who picks the flowers represents right concentration that unifies the mind. But to unify the mind and eliminate all distractions and defilements, concentration needs to be supported by the right effort of the boy upon whom he stands, and to be stabilized by the right mindfulness represented by the third boy.

The fundamental support for meditation practice is thus right effort. Time and time again, the Buddha stressed the need for determined effort, diligence, and unflagging perseverance to cleanse the mind of unwholesome states and to cultivate the wholesome ones. Still, he recognized that it is possible to try too hard. He used the example of a musical instrument. If you tighten the strings too much when tuning it, they break. But if you don't tighten them enough, they won't make any sound. Thus, right effort is not just a matter of hard work but also a balance between extremes, just as the entire path follows the middle way between indulgence and self-mortification.

The next factor, right mindfulness, is also translated as "right memory" or "right awareness." To have right mindfulness is to constantly remember to maintain a steady attentive awareness of the present moment without judgment, interpretation, or any other kind of mental elaboration. If such distractions occur, they are simply noted and allowed to dissolve back into the sea of calm awareness.

Right concentration is the last factor on the eightfold path. The Buddha said that the untrained mind was like a fish flopping around on land after it has been pulled from the water—it can't stay put but twists and turns from thought to thought without direction or control. Right concentration is simply to put one's attention on a single object and keep it there without flopping around.

The Path of the Buddha's Enlightenment

In many of the sutras, the Buddha's teachings on the eightfold path are like the bullets in a PowerPoint presentation—they only hit the key points. They need more elaboration before they can effectively be put into practice, and that is especially true when it comes to his meditation instructions. Other sutras offer more detailed instructions, but they provide us with something of an embarrassment of riches. The Buddha was a genius at tailoring his instructions to the needs of each individual who questioned him, but as a result he left us with so many different and sometimes contradictory directions that it is hard to know which ones to follow. Later commentators developed different systems of practice based on his original teachings, but there are many ways in which they do not agree. So which path do the teachings of the first turning recommend? For our purposes at least, I think it is best to turn to the path the Buddha himself followed. Not only is it described in one form or another in numerous different sutras, but he explicitly held it up as an example for his monks to follow.[20]

According to the teachings of the first turning, the only difference between the path of the Buddha and that of his followers was that the

Buddha had to discover it for himself while his disciples had a teacher who had already laid it out for them.[21] The Buddha began his historic journey to enlightenment when, overcome by the suffering of the world, he left home and became a wandering striver seeking a way to free himself and all suffering beings. In many of the teachings of the first turning, such as the *Kandaraka Sutta*,[22] the Buddha describes a slightly different motivation for his followers that wasn't possible for him: faith in the Buddha and what he teaches.

Once someone was inspired by hearing the Dharma, the first step the Buddha recommended both in his words and by his example was that a sincere seeker of liberation "go forth into homelessness"—that is, become a monk. As the Buddha puts it in the *Kandaraka Sutta*:

> On hearing the Dhamma he [a layperson] acquires faith in the Tathagata. Possessing that faith, he considers thus: "Household life is crowded and dusty; life gone forth is wide open. It is not easy, while living in a home, to lead the holy life utterly perfect and pure as a polished shell. Suppose I shave off my hair and beard, put on the yellow robe, and go forth from the home life into homelessness."[23]

While the Buddha himself didn't become a monk during his spiritual quest, since there was obviously no monastic community yet, he practiced a regime of renunciation and strict discipline that became the inspiration for the formal rules he offered to the monastic sangha he created. By following strict monastic discipline free from the distractions of family life, these strivers purify themselves and lay the groundwork for the next stage on the path. The monk abstains from all sexual activities, from all killing and violence, and from false or malicious speech. He only eats one meal a day and does not sing, dance, or listen to music. As a result of such austerities, he learns to stop grasping at sense experience and becomes content, mindful, and fully aware of what he is doing.

After leaving home on this path of renunciation, the Buddha himself studied with two great meditation teachers of his time. Unlike most of us, he was able to quickly give up the five hindrances to meditation—sensual desire, ill will, sloth and torpor, restlessness and remorse, and doubt—and master the progressively deeper stages of meditative absorption known as the *jhanas*. And this is the same path the Buddha recommends to his monks:

> On returning from his almsround, after his meal he [a monk] sits down, folding his legs crosswise, setting his body erect, and establishing mindfulness before him . . . Having thus abandoned these five hindrances . . . he enters upon and abides in the first jhana . . . the second jhana . . . the third jhana . . . the fourth jhana . . .[24]

Each of the four jhanas *Kandaraka Sutta* lists embodies progressively deeper states of concentration. However, some other sutras list four additional states of meditative absorption, bringing the total to eight.

This style of meditation has come to be known as *shamatha* or tranquility meditation, and the basic technique is really quite simple. You select an object of meditation and put all your attention on that one point. Interestingly, the sutras don't tell us what object the Buddha used, but they do record him recommending many different objects of meditation to his students: the colored disks known as *kasinas*, the four "divine abodes" (loving-kindness, compassion, sympathetic joy, and equanimity), and the object most commonly used by meditators today—the breath. Whichever object the meditator uses, the results are often the same. As their concentration improves, their thoughts still, their minds settle down, and they experience progressively more refined states that involve such things as rapture, joy, and equanimity.

Unlike the other teachers of his time, however, the Buddha realized that however wonderful these states, they are impermanent and do not offer a final end to suffering. For that, we must turn to the practice of what has come to be known as *vipassana* or insight meditation: using the concentrated mind developed through shamatha to gain direct insight into the way things really are.

On the night of his great enlightenment, the Buddha first practiced the jhanas and then turned to vipassana and the recollection of his past lives:

> When my concentrated mind was thus purified, bright, unblemished, rid of imperfection malleable, wieldy, steady, and attained to imperturbability, I directed it to knowledge of the recollection of past lives.[25]

Next, he turned his attention to karma, and the birth, death, and rebirth of beings.

> With the divine eye, which is purified and surpasses the human, I saw beings passing away and reappearing, inferior and superior, fair and ugly, fortunate and unfortunate. I understood how beings pass on according to their actions . . ."[26]

He saw that those who live good lives have a favorable rebirth, and those who live evil lives suffer grave consequences. Finally, the Buddha reached the final stage that led to his complete liberation:

> When my concentrated mind was thus purified . . . I directed it to knowledge of the destruction of the taints . . . I directly knew as it actually is: "This is the origin of suffering"; I directly knew as it actually is: "This is the cessation of suffering"; I directly knew as it actually is: "This is the way leading to the cessation of suffering."

In other words, he directly realized the four noble truths. He goes on:

> When I knew and saw thus, my mind was liberated from the taint of sensual desire, from the taint of being, and from the taint of ignorance . . . I directly knew: "Birth is destroyed, the holy life has been lived, what had to be done has been done, there is no more coming to any state of being."[27]

The Buddha had realized nirvana and the freedom from rebirth into the world of suffering.

Other sutras give more detailed lists of what can be contemplated in vipassana meditation. The most influential is the great *Satipatthana*

Sutta (*Sutra on the Foundations of Mindfulness*), which is not only the foundation for many classic meditation practices but also an inspiration for the mindfulness movement that is gaining such popularity in the West. The sutra never mentions the practice of the jhanas, but starts off with instructions for following the breath, which is the object typically used in shamatha meditation, and goes on to give many different types of vipassana meditations in four main groups.[28] It starts with contemplations of the body that include the breath, posture, and the general repulsiveness of the body. Then it proceeds to contemplations of the feelings and of the mind. Finally, there are the contemplations of the dharmas or mind objects, which start with the hindrances mentioned above and culminate with the four noble truths.

The breath, the body, or the mind and its formations can be an object of either shamatha or vipassana, so what is different between the two? To practice shamatha with any object is simply to focus all one's attention on it. In vipassana, however, we seek to investigate those objects and see them exactly as the really are. And as Bhikkhu Bodhi puts it: "To see things as they really are means to see them in terms of the three characteristics—as impermanent, as painful or suffering, and as not self."[29] When we directly and fully realize that all human experience is impermanent, unsatisfactory, and without any kind of independent self behind it, we are free from all attachment and attain full liberation.

The entire corpus of teachings and commentaries that make up the first turning of the wheel can fill a library. But they are, in essence, fairly simple, straightforward teachings with a kind of scientific quality. Just like a medical text, a problem is identified (suffering), its cause (craving) is described, and the means to cure it (the eightfold path) are clearly spelled out. The cure is a path of renunciation that leads to freedom from the constant cycle of death and rebirth and entanglement with worldly life. If practitioners dedicate themselves to the progressive development of wisdom, ethical conduct, and meditation, the goal of nirvana will surely be achieved and the end to suffering will be at hand.

The Second Turning
of the Wheel: Emptiness

The second turning of the wheel must have come as a bombshell to the Buddhist world. It not only threatened to blow apart the conventional understanding of the Buddhist path, but it challenged just about everything else we know and believe as well. The sutras tell the story of the stunned reactions of the monks when the Buddha first gave these teachings to an assembly of his most enlightened disciples. Some apparently thought he had gone crazy and walked out, while others were so shocked they were said to have had heart attacks, vomited blood, and died.[30] What was in these teachings that could possibly arouse such a reaction? These were, and still remain, expressions of the most radical wisdom that in a very real sense threaten to wipe out the world as we understand it. They tell us that all our comforting beliefs, whether they concern Buddhism, science, culture, or anything else, and even our habitual habits of perception, must be left behind if we are to cross over to the other side and leave the river of suffering. It was a message that many of the monks who had spent their lives on the path of discipline and arduous training outlined in the teachings of the first turning of the wheel simply could not accept. How could the four noble truths, the eightfold path, and everything else they believed in be nothing but empty words?

Although the teachings of the second turning were probably around in one form or another a long time before they were first written down, we do have fragments of text from around the first century BCE—some four hundred years after the Buddha's death. Those centuries following the Buddha's death had seen a fundamental transformation in Indian society and in the religion he founded. A huge agricultural empire had come and gone and many competing kingdoms dotted the Indian landscape. With the spread of trade and commerce, writing came into common use, and the level of cultural sophistication escalated exponentially. Many of the early Buddhist encampments had grown up to become large monasteries, a few of which were eventually to turn into great universities. Buddhism itself had gone from being a challenger of the orthodoxy to a powerful established religion with a large body of full-time monastics, royal patronage, and an orthodoxy of its own.

Such a radical shift in sociological position brought many advantages to organized Buddhism, but it brought some inevitable spiritual problems as well. It seems clear from the comments of their critics that despite the Buddha's repeated warnings not to become attached to his teachings, many monks had done just that and had moreover come to see themselves as a kind of spiritual elite standing above the average people. Early Mahayana sutras attacked monks who were "intent on acquisitions and honors," as well as those who had wives and children or who owned cattle, horses, and slaves.[31]

The advocates of the second turning of the wheel sought, among other things, to pull the rug out from under the Buddhist establishment, or at least from under those members of the establishment who had grown proud and complacent. The historical record is sketchy and incomplete and scholars continue to argue about it, but it appears that until the growth of the Pala Empire in the eighth century of the common era, the advocates of the second turning remained outsiders from the Buddhist establishment of India, calling for change from the forests and small marginalized monastic groups. In contrast, these new teachings probably caught on much earlier in East Asia where they did not have to compete with already entrenched opponents.[32]

The Prajnaparamita

The teachings that set the second turning of the wheel in motion have come down to us in a large group of sutras and commentaries known collectively as the *prajnaparamita* literature. Like so many concepts in the Buddhist tradition, prajnaparamita has more than one meaning. *Prajna* is usually translated as wisdom, but it is easy to get confused if we assume that *prajna* is used in the same way as *wisdom* is typically used in the West. *Prajna* refers to a more fundamental wisdom than the knowledge we gain by reading books or reflecting on the meaning of life or the nature of the world. It is a direct insight into the true nature of things that is beyond our words, concepts, or beliefs.

Many commentators have pointed out that *paramita* has two possible derivations in Sanskrit and thus two possible meanings. *Parama* refers to the highest point and *paramita* is perfection. So the most common translation of prajnaparamita is "the perfection of wisdom." Thus, these sutras are seen to be wisdom in its highest, most perfect manifestation. On the other hand, *paramita* can also be seen to be a combination of the Sanskrit word *para* that means beyond, and *ita* that means gone. Thus, *paramita* means "what has gone beyond" or "what is transcendent." So from this perspective, the *prajnaparamita* is transcendent wisdom that surpasses ordinary wisdom. Obviously, the meanings of these two translations are not all that different, but I think transcendent wisdom comes a little closer to the mark, since the implication that wisdom can be perfected seems to increase our risk of turning it into just another object of our attachment.

To complicate the matter a bit more, because *ita* is feminine, *prajnaparamita* can also be read as "she who has gone beyond" or "she who leads us to the other shore."[33] In fact, Prajnaparamita is commonly envisioned as a great female goddess. But the feminine form she takes is not just a mater of etymology. When it is seen to have any qualities at all, this great transcendent wisdom is truly feminine. She is the mother of the buddhas who gives birth to the wisdom that sets us free, and as such she has been an inspiration and object of devotion to countless generations of Buddhists. I know many of us raised in the Western rationalist tradition

grow rather uncomfortable when we hear that a sutra is somehow transformed into a goddess, but hopefully this strange transformation will
make more sense by the end of this chapter.

For now, consider this passage from Lex Hixon's loose translation of
the *Prajnaparamita in 8,000 Lines*. This ancient hymn gives us a moving
expression of the sense of devotion this goddess inspires:

> I sing this spontaneous hymn of light to praise Mother
> Prajnaparamita . . . She is utterly unstained, because nothing in
> this insubstantial world can possibly stain her. She is an ever-
> flowing fountain of incomparable light, and from every conscious
> being on every plane, she removes the faintest trace of illusory
> darkness . . . In her alone can we find true refuge . . . She clearly
> and constantly points out the path of wisdom to every conscious
> being . . . Mother Prajnaparamita is total awakeness . . . She is the
> Perfect Wisdom which never comes into being and therefore never
> goes out of being . . . She can never be defeated in any way, on
> any level. She lovingly protects vulnerable conscious beings who
> cannot protect themselves, gradually generating in them unshak-
> able fearlessness and diamond confidence . . . Her transcendent
> knowing never waivers. She is the Perfect Wisdom who gives birth-
> less birth to all Buddhas. And through these sublimely Awakened
> Ones, it is Mother Prajnaparamita alone who turns the wheel of
> true teaching.[34]

The *Diamond Sutra*

Although it only dates from the ninth century, the oldest printed and
dated book in the world is arguably a Chinese edition of the *Diamond
Sutra* held by the British Museum. The sutra itself has, of course, been
around for a lot longer. In fact, the *Diamond Sutra* is probably the oldest
of all the prajnaparamita sutras.[35]

In most Western translations the *Diamond Sutra* has twenty-five to
thirty very densely packed pages, while many of the numerous commentaries run to hundreds of pages. Fortunately, like most texts that were

originally memorized rather than written down, the *Diamond Sutra* contains a lot of repetition, and our goal will be to focus on a few central themes that it hits again and again, which form the heart of the teachings of the second turning of the wheel.

Like so many other Buddhist sutras, the *Diamond that Cuts Though Illusion* (another of this sutra's names), begins with a description of the setting in which the Buddha gave his teachings. The Buddha lived a wandering life, and when he gave these teachings, he was staying in a park in the middle of a forest donated by one of his followers, accompanied by over a thousand of his monks.

One morning after he did his begging rounds and ate his meal, one of his greatest disciples approached him. He was called Subhuti, born of emptiness, and he bowed respectfully and asked a portentous question. "What should someone who wishes to follow the bodhisattva path and attain complete enlightenment do to master his mind?" Subhuti's question shows that he was still thinking in the logical systematic terms of the first turning: it assumes there is a path one can follow, that enlightenment awaits at its end, and the way to get there is through mastery of the mind.

The Buddha's response and the dialogue that follows destroy that way of thinking blow by blow:

> Subhuti, those who would now set forth on the bodhisattva path should thus give birth to the following thought: "However many beings there are in whatever realms of being that might exist, whether they are born from an egg or born from a womb, born from the water or born from the air, whether they have form or no form . . . I shall liberate them all."[36]

The sutras of the first turning of the wheel seldom use the term *bodhisattva*, and when they do, it refers only to the Buddha before he had attained enlightenment. But the Buddha starts off this sutra using the term in a completely different way, one that provides a radical new vision of Buddhist practice. The teachings of the first turning always instructed the Buddha's followers to be loving, kind, and compassionate toward all

living beings, but the goal of Buddhist practice was to attain nirvana—
the complete end of all personal suffering and with it the end of rebirth
into this world. But here the Buddha tells Subhuti that those who wish
to follow the bodhisattva path should dedicate themselves to the liberation of all sentient beings, not just themselves. Of course, the bodhisattva is herself a sentient being deserving of liberation, but as many other
sutras make clear, the bodhisattva vows to forgo release into the bliss
of nirvana until all other beings have been saved. It is the power of this
great aspiration that drives the seeker down the bodhisattva path, and
it represents a fundamental pivot in the orientation of Buddhist practice
from the "other-worldly" goal of nirvana to the "worldly" concern with
the liberation of all beings.

As if that wasn't enough dynamite, the Buddha drops an even bigger
bombshell in the very next sentence:

> And when this innumerable, immeasurable, infinite number of
> beings have been liberated, no beings have in truth been liberated.

The great bodhisattva vow may sound too impossibly lofty to ever
achieve, but at least it is pretty easy to understand. But what in the world
does the Buddha mean here? How can this huge number of beings have
been liberated, if no beings have been liberated? It just doesn't seem to
make sense.

The Buddha goes on to explain:

> And why not? Subhuti, no one can be called a bodhisattva who cre-
> ates the perception of a self or who creates a perception of a being,
> a life, or a soul.[37]

Different commentators understand these profound and mysterious
teachings in different ways, but it does seem clear that the Buddha is,
at least in part, reaffirming the doctrine of anatman or no-self that he
asserted in so many places in the sutras of the first turning. Aside from
self, *atman* is also the Hindu word for soul, so the Buddha is obviously
rejecting the Hindu belief in a soul or in some independently existing

essence at the core of the individual. But he also seems to go much farther than that when he rejects the ideas of a person, a being, or a life, since those terms don't necessarily imply the existence of such an independent self or soul.

Although the full implications of this teaching were not explicitly spelled out until the third turning of the wheel, when Buddha says a bodhisattva does not believe in the *idea* of a self, person, being, or life, I think he was challenging our belief in ideas themselves. Our ideas of a self, a person, a being, a life, or for that matter anything else are simply creations of our mind. If we confuse our ideas about reality with reality itself, we become lost in a sea of suffering and confusion. We use our ideas to create a simplified picture of the world that gives us the illusion that we understand what is going on and can control it. But the fact is that our ideas, concepts, and beliefs are exactly that—ideas, concepts, and beliefs. They are not the world that we so desperately try to grasp. According to the *Flower Ornament Sutra*, even the simplest mote of dust contains the entire universe and cannot be confined by our limited understanding. The belief that any words or concepts can grasp reality is a fundamental delusion lying at the root of all human suffering.

But if there aren't really any sentient beings, why does the Buddha tell us that aspiring bodhisattvas should dedicate themselves to liberating them? The answer is, of course, that dedicating oneself and one's life to the liberation of all beings everywhere is a profound, wonderful, and wholesome thing to do that brings vast benefit to the world. But only, as the Buddha points out, if we don't become attached to those ideas and start believing there really are any suffering beings or some kind of independent "me" that is liberating them. The idea that you might liberate all suffering beings is only a dream, but it is a beautiful and a beneficial dream, and we need such dreams to guide us along the way.

By this point, the Buddha's audience of dedicated followers was probably getting a little confused, for this is a deep and difficult wisdom, but I doubt that anyone was vomiting blood and collapsing yet. The rest of this great sutra works and reworks these themes to make their implications more clear, and as the true meaning of these profound revelations dawned on his audience, things undoubtedly changed. In chapter 14 of the *Diamond Sutra*, the Buddha explicitly recognizes how extraordinarily difficult these teachings are to accept: "If there are people who are able to hear this sutra, and are not startled, terrified, or fearful, know that the existence of such a person is extremely rare." Why are these teachings so terrifying? Because they pull the rug out from under everything we depend on, even the teachings themselves.

As in the sutras of the first turning, the Buddha tells us explicitly that however helpful the teachings are, sooner or later they have to be abandoned. In chapter 6 the Buddha tells his monks that:

> Bhikshus, you should know that all the teachings I give you are like a raft. All teachings must be abandoned, not to mention the non-teachings.[38]

In other words, the teachings are a raft to ferry us across the river of suffering to the shores of liberation, but once we get across, we no longer need the raft and it must be abandoned. If we cling to the teachings as some kind of ultimate truth, then our attachment will make us suffer. In chapter 21, the Buddha makes the point even more strongly when he tells Subhuti:

> Subhuti, do not say it ever occurs to the Tathagata that "I teach the dharma." If anyone says that the Tathagata has something to teach, that person slanders the Tathagata.

If just calling the Buddha a teacher slanders him, we are left without the slightest shred of security or certainty that there is anything to gain from listening to him, and that is exactly what the Buddha intended.

And just as we must avoid making the Buddha or his teachings into an object of our attachment, we must also avoid making ourselves into an object with various signs and characteristics. As mentioned above, the Buddha explicitly warned us not to look at ourselves as a self, person, being, or as having a life, or attributing any of those characteristics to other beings. Even more deadly to our spiritual practice is the belief that we have attained something from that practice or that we have some kind of special spiritual qualities that others don't. As Subhuti tells the Buddha:

> The Buddha has often said that I am foremost among his disciples in the meditation of peaceful abiding and that I am the one most free of desire. However, I do not have the thought "I am free of desire." If I did the Buddha would not speak of me as "Subhuti who dwells in peace." Because there is no dwelling he speaks of me as "Subhuti who dwells in peace."

Again and again in this sutra, the Buddha presents us with a wall that seems completely impenetrable to reason or logic. In the early chapters, we learn that although the Buddha liberates countless beings, no beings are liberated and that the attributes possessed by the Buddha are not attributes. But this logic of denial takes an even more puzzling turn later in the sutra beginning with this passage in chapter 8:

> "What do you think Subhuti? If someone filled billions of worlds with jewels and offered them as a gift of generosity, would the merit gained be great?" And Subhuti answered, "Yes it would be great indeed, because whatever is said by the Tathagata to be great merit, is not great merit, thus the Tathagata calls it great merit."

This same logical claim, A is not A and therefore it is called A, is repeated time and again throughout the rest of the sutra. We hear that creating a serene and beautiful buddhafield is not creating a serene and beautiful buddhafield and therefore it is called creating a serene and beautiful buddhafield; that the highest transcendent wisdom in not the highest transcendent wisdom and therefore it is called the highest transcendent wisdom; that particles of dust are not particles of dust and therefore they are truly particles of dust; and on and on.

How can we make sense of this kind of crazy logic? Commentators have, of course, offered many explanations over the centuries. It is common, for example, to claim that when the Buddha said that some object, say a particle of dust, is not in fact a particle of dust, he meant that it has no distinct separate essence (or "own being" to use the technical Buddhist term), but exists only in dependence on innumerable other causes and conditions beyond itself. Then when he goes on to say that a particle of dust is a particle of dust because it isn't a particle of dust, what he means is that it would not really be possible for a particle of dust to exist if it had some fixed independent essence. If it did, it would be totally unchanging and separate from the rest of the world, and thus would not be like a real particle of dust at all. Therefore, the fact that it is not a (independently existing) particle of dust enables it to be a particle of dust. This kind of argument may sound a little tortured, but it is not only very much in line with Buddhist tradition, it offers us a great nugget of profound wisdom.

Nonetheless, looking at the sutra with fresh twenty-first-century eyes, we have to wonder why the Buddha would have said that "a particle of dust is not a particle of dust and therefore we call it a particle of dust," if he really wanted to say that "a particle of dust lacks any independent essence"? Why didn't he just say that, if that is what he meant? Perhaps the need for interpretation itself is the problem. Although the temptation to try to analyze and explain such puzzling statements is almost irresistible for commentators, scholars, and practitioners alike, we need to be open to the possibility that the Buddha didn't intend that it be interpreted in neat conceptual categories and that its mystery implies far more than could ever be spelled out it words.

This might be a good spot to pull back and ask yourself, "How am I responding to these teachings?" "What am I feeling right now?" On first hearing most people will probably be a little puzzled about what these teachings mean or perhaps even reject them out of hand as completely nonsensical. Even those who have some kind of surface-level intellectual understanding may start to feel the fear and anxiety the Buddha mentioned as the deeper meaning really starts to sink in. Once again the temptation is to reject the whole thing and find another teaching that can provide a sense of security and a clear-cut conceptual framework to cling to. But there is another possible reaction if you can get beyond the resistance and penetrate to the core of this great wisdom. Chapter 14 describes Subhuti's response to the teaching:

The venerable Subhuti was moved to tears by the force of this teaching. Wiping his eyes, he said to the Buddha, "How rare in this world, how remarkable is this teaching. I have never heard such wonderful teachings before! Those who hear what is said in this sutra and give birth to a perception of its truth are the most remarkably blessed of bodhisattvas."

Then, of course, Subhuti finishes off by once again pulling the rug out from under us:

And how so? Bhagavan [another of the Buddha's many names], a perception of truth is no perception of truth, thus it is called a perception of truth.

The *Heart Sutra*

As you read these lines, someone somewhere in the world is probably chanting the *Heart Sutra*. It may well be the most popular and best known of the thousands of scriptures in the Buddhist Canon, and its declaration that "form is emptiness, emptiness is form" certainly ranks among the most famous statements in all Buddhism. Its full title is often given as the *Prajnaparamita Hridaya Sutra: Heart of Perfect Wisdom* or *Heart of the Prajnaparamita*. Although it is only a page long, it does indeed express the heart of the prajnaparamita literature, and many commentators consider it to contain all the vast wisdom of that tradition.

Like so much in Buddhism, its origins are a matter of scholarly dispute. Red Pine says it was probably composed in the first century of the common era, the great Japanese scholar Nakamura Hajime puts it in the second century, Edward Conze in the fourth, while Jan Nattier doubts it could be dated earlier than the seventh century. What they do all agree on is that it is indeed a summary of prajnaparamita literature. In fact, large portions of the *Heart Sutra* appear to be taken directly from the much larger *Perfection of Wisdom in 25,000 Lines*. Indeed, Nattier has suggested that the original version of the *Heart Sutra* was actually composed in China from a mixture of Indian-derived material and new composition, and was only later translated back into Sanskrit.[39]

As you might expect from so condensed a text, the very first line of the *Heart Sutra* goes right to the heart of the teachings:

> While practicing deeply the prajnaparamita, the bodhisattva Avalokiteshvara perceived that all five skandhas are empty and broke the bonds that caused him suffering.

To those who are not familiar with Buddhism, this sentence takes a little unpacking. First off, the central character in this sutra, Avalokiteshvara, is one of the most revered figures in all of Mahayana Buddhism. He is a bodhisattva, which, as the *Diamond Sutra* tells us, means that he has dedicated himself to the liberation of all beings. But unlike most seekers on the path, he is so advanced that he is virtually indistinguishable from a full-fledged buddha. Indeed, the shorter of the two versions of the *Heart Sutra* is one of the few sutras in which the Buddha doesn't even appear.[40] Avalokiteshvara means something like "the lord who gazes down on the suffering of the world" or "the lord who hears the cries of the world," and he is considered to be the living embodiment of compassion. In East Asia, he changed genders and became the beautiful female figure of Kwan Yin who graces so much great Chinese art, and he is considered by many Tibetans to be the guardian of their country.

So this great compassionate bodhisattva is "practicing deeply the prajnaparamita," in other words meditating, and he has a great breakthrough. He sees that all five *skandhas* are empty, and that great realization ends his suffering once and for all. So what is a skandha? As we saw in the previous chapter, the Buddha says that a human being and all human experience are made up of five aggregates or heaps of momentary events (dharmas); these aggregates are the skandhas. They are in some sense the limits of reality and include all possible experiences. The teachings of the first turning tell us that what we mistakenly cling to as an independently existing self is nothing but a collection of these five aggregates: forms, feelings, perceptions, mental formations, and consciousness. In reality, there is no self to cling to, just a stream of passing experiences.

In the first turning, these momentary passing experiences that aggregate into the skandhas are the only true reality. Here, however, Avalokiteshvara goes a step farther and tells us that even the skandhas and the dharmas that make them up are themselves completely empty.

The next question is, obviously, what is emptiness? That is, to say the least, a daunting question. But the answer is an important one, because although the term was never used in the *Diamond Sutra* and only rarely in the sutras of the first turning, over the centuries it became one of the most central concepts in all Mahayana Buddhism.

The *Heart Sutra* doesn't give us a direct answer, but you could fill a library with the answers provided by the commentators. Some versions of the *Heart Sutra* do, however, provide us with a hint; after Avalokiteshvara's revelation that "all five skandhas are empty," some add a phrase like "of own being" or "of self-nature." Thus, the realization that things are empty is the realization that they lack any kind of independent essence or "own nature." Unfortunately, few people have much of an idea what "own being" or "self-nature" means. The concept comes from technical Buddhist philosophy that holds that the roots of suffering can be traced to the erroneous belief that the objects we perceive have some kind of independent essence (*svabhava* in Sanskrit) that makes them what they are. A tree, for example, is believed to have an essence of "treeness" that is completely independent of its surroundings, but the truth is that it is empty of any such treeness.

We don't, however, have to penetrate the depths of technical Buddhist philosophy to get an idea of what Avalokiteshvara meant when he said that everything we perceive is empty. If things are empty, then they are hollow, ephemeral, and without substance. While they may appear solid and stable, that is just an illusion, and the lives we build on a foundation of illusion inevitably lead us to suffering. In fact, the things that appear to us are just that: appearances and nothing more. Although it never uses the term, the *Diamond Sutra* provides a potent expression of emptiness in this famous little verse:

As phantom, a star in space,
an illusion, a dewdrop, a bubble,
a dream, a cloud, a flash of lightning,
Thus are all created things to be regarded.

The next lines in the *Heart Sutra* pound home the same point.

Oh Shariputra,
form is emptiness, emptiness is form,
form is not other than emptiness,
emptiness not other than form,
that which is form is emptiness,
that which is emptiness is form.

The same is true for feelings, perceptions, mental formations,
and consciousness.

In the teachings of the first turning, Shariputra is often considered the Buddha's foremost disciple. In fact, several of the talks recorded in the Pali Canon were given by Shariputra and not the Buddha himself. The fact that the great bodhisattva Avalokiteshvara addresses these lines to Shariputra can be seen as an effort to get him to realize the emptiness and insubstantiality of the teachings of the first turning that he was so skillful in relating.

Form is usually given as the first of the skandhas, and Avalokiteshvara clearly uses it as a stand-in for all five, since he only briefly mentions the other four at the end of this passage. Therefore, in one sense he is merely restating what he said in the previous passage: that the skandhas are all empty. But the passage means much more than that, and there is good reason that Avalokiteshvara's declaration that "Form is emptiness, emptiness is form" is so famous.

Rather than trying to analyze this statement, at first it is probably better to just repeat it to ourselves and feel the power of the words. Somehow they speak to the depths of understanding that go far beyond any conceptual meaning.

When we do turn ourselves to the intellectual understanding of what the words mean, it quickly becomes obvious that "form is emptiness" surrenders its meaning to us far more easily than "emptiness is form." As we have seen, "form is emptiness" implies that form and by extension all the other skandhas are empty, hollow, and insubstantial. They have no solid independent existence. Although this sutra never says it directly, some commentators even claim that emptiness simply means interdependence: nothing is independent or self-sustaining but in fact depends for its existence on everything else in the universe in an infinite web of mutual causality. Or using the common definition of emptiness we mentioned above, we can read this passage as saying that all things lack an independent essence or "own being" that makes them what they are. In other words, all compounded things are, as the *Diamond Sutra* tells us, like a phantom, a dewdrop, a dream, a flash of lightning in the sky.

While it is fairly easy to understand how a form such as a tree might lack any kind of independent solidity or true defining essence, what does it mean to say emptiness is form? How can the lack of any independent solidity or defining essence *be* a tree? If we stick with the definition of emptiness as being merely the absence of something, then the idea that "emptiness is form" doesn't seem to make much sense, for it appears impossible for the mere absence of something—be it substantiality, independence, essence, or anything else—to be a tree.

It is, however, possible to see emptiness in more positive terms. The great Zen Buddhist scholar D.T. Suzuki called it the Absolute, while more traditional Buddhist thought employs such terms as buddha nature or suchness. But to see emptiness as some kind of mysterious undivided wholeness that is the source of all being and nonbeing is a controversial move in Buddhism. Although that is the predominant view in the teachings of the third turning, critics including many of those in the Gelukpa sect of Tibetan Buddhism, to which the Dalai Lama belongs, warn that the concept of buddha nature can be a back-door way to reintroduce the idea of a self into Buddhism. Yet while the danger of clinging to a reified conception of emptiness is a real one, the conclusion that this famous passage points to something more than just an absence, but rather some kind of awakened buddha nature or Absolute, is hard to avoid.

The next passage in the sutra is also addressed to Shariputra:

Oh Shariputra, dharmas are characterized by emptiness. They are neither produced nor destroyed. They are not pure nor defiled. They neither increase nor decrease.

Interestingly, aside from being a leading exponent of the teachings of the first wheel, Shariputra is also considered by some to be the one who compiled the earliest version of the Abhidharma—an effort to organize and systematize the teachings of the Buddha and create a comprehensive list of all the different kinds of momentary events, which were believed to be the buildings blocks of experience—and here Avalokiteshvara is clearly challenging one of its most basic beliefs. The most common view among the monks who studied the Abhidharma was that people lacked a self or independent reality because they were nothing but a constantly changing stream of these momentary events or dharmas, yet they felt that the dharmas themselves were in fact real and substantial. But here Avalokiteshvara tells Shariputra that not only are the skandhas empty, but so are the dharmas that make them up.

In their essence, dharmas are pure emptiness, and like emptiness itself they have no beginning or end, they are neither defiled nor pure, they do not increase or decrease. Avalokiteshvara is also denying the basic Buddhist doctrine of impermanence here, since if something has no beginning and no end, it cannot in any real sense be said to be impermanent. Of course, even though it doesn't specifically say so here, there is no doubt that Avalokiteshvara would also deny that things are permanent. When Avalokiteshvara says that dharmas are neither tainted nor pure, he rejects the efforts of those who focus their practice on purifying themselves of the defilements (*kleshas*) such as greed, hatred, and delusion. If there are no defiled states, it is obviously a waste of time to try to get rid of them.

Next come the negations, a series of crashing hammer blows, often chanted with a rhythmic beat, that seek nothing less than to bring down the world as we know it and all the remaining Buddhist teachings with it.

Therefore Shariputra, in emptiness there is no form, no feelings, no
perceptions, no mental formations, and no consciousness.

So once again, Avalokiteshvara denies the reality of the five skandhas.

No eyes, no ears, no nose, no tongue, no body, no mind,
No shapes, no sound, no smell, no taste, no touch, no objects of
mind,
No realms of perceptual awareness from eye to mind consciousness.

Here Avalokiteshvara denies all the elements of the Buddhist theory
of perception, which holds that the contact of a sense organ, like an
eye, with a sense object, like a shape, produces a sense consciousness
or perception, which in this example would be an "eye consciousness."
Buddhist theory starts with the same five senses as Western psychology, but also includes the mind as a sixth sense, and all of them are
specifically denied in the first line of this passage. In the next line, the
six objects of the senses are in turn each denied, and the last line denies
each of the six realms of perceptual awareness.

The twelvefold chain of dependent origination that some who follow
the first turning of the wheel see as a perfect summary of the Buddha's
teachings is Avalokiteshvara's next target.

No links of dependent origination and no end of them
from ignorance to death and decay.

Avalokiteshvara then turns his sights on the innermost core of the
Buddha's teachings:

No suffering, no cause of suffering, no end of suffering, no noble
path that leads from suffering.

Thus, he denies the four noble truths and the eightfold path that
the Buddha set forth in his very first sermon. While a lot of the monks

gathered around to hear these teaching may have already been pretty uncomfortable, I think this is the time they must have started running out or falling over and vomiting blood on the ground.

These amazing passages are something truly unique in all the world's religious literature. What other tradition has ever openly denied all its own basic doctrines? It is as if the last book of the Bible said there was no God, or Mohammed had said that the Koran was not holy and that he was not the messenger of God. It seems almost unthinkable, but here it is. And of course, that is exactly the point. Anything that is thinkable, even the great teachings of the Buddha, is only words and concepts, and words and concepts can never capture reality.

Just in case he left anything out, Avalokiteshvara ends his string of negations by adding "No wisdom, no attainment, and no nonattainment." Wisdom is often said to be the basic goal of the whole Buddhist path, but if there is no wisdom, then obviously there is nothing to be obtained by Buddhist practice. By denying that we can attain anything from Buddhist practice, Avalokiteshvara takes sides in a debate that is just as hot among today's Buddhists as it was two thousand years ago. Some feel that the goal of Buddhist practice is the sublime state of nirvana that can be reached by diligently studying the Buddha's teachings and by practicing meditation and virtuous behavior in order to purify the obstructions that block the way to the goal. Others feel that because there is no self or any other separate distinct entities, the whole idea that one could attain something is pure ego-centered delusion. In this view, we are now and have always been nothing but pure luminous emptiness. The only problem is that we don't realize it.

With the traditional Buddhist understanding of the world in rubble at his feet, Avalokiteshvara suddenly pivots to reaffirm the way of the bodhisattva.

With no attainment the bodhisattvas dwell in the perfect wisdom
of the prajnaparamita and find no obstacles for their minds.

Having no obstacles they have no fear, and they see through all
delusion, final nirvana.[41]

The bodhisattvas let go of any notion of wisdom, attainment, or nonattainment. They let go of absolutely everything, and rest in the perfect wisdom of the prajnaparamita, that is to say, in emptiness. Resting in emptiness, there are no obstacles for their minds. No matter how bad, their circumstances no longer pose the slightest barrier. Even the most harmful passions arise and pass away without leaving a mark, and the walls of delusion melt away. Once a bodhisattva can endure the total groundlessness of her life, she is liberated from all fear and sees things exactly as they are. This is the final nirvana.

> All buddhas of the past, present, and future abide in the prajnaparamita and realize complete unsurpassed perfect enlightenment.

Avalokiteshvara tells us that all buddhas are born from Prajnaparamita, which is why the *Perfection of Wisdom in 8,000 Lines* calls her "the mother of the buddhas." There is no other path, no other way. Complete unsurpassed perfect enlightenment requires the realization of the luminous emptiness that is the perfection of wisdom. The arhats who root out all their desires and defilements have obtained a great spiritual achievement, but true buddhahood goes beyond any achievement or any thought that there is such a thing as nirvana or that one has realized it.

We can imagine that Avalokiteshvara must have shaken Shariputra to his very core, for among all the Buddha's followers Shariputra had the most brilliant intellectual understanding of the teachings of the first turning. This complete and utter destruction of all intellectual understanding must have been a painful and difficult thing for him and most of the other monks as well. What are they to do after the careful systematic path to liberation they were following dissolves into emptiness? They were told to just rest in that emptiness, but that isn't much consolation for those thirsting for an instruction book to show them the way to freedom.

What Avalokiteshvara does provide is a mantra:

> Therefore you should know the great mantra of the prajnaparamita. The great bright mantra, the utmost mantra, the supreme

mantra that heals all suffering and is true not false. So proclaim the Prajnaparamita Mantra, the mantra that says:

Gate, gate, paragate, parasamgate, bodhi svaha.

Mantras sometimes have a literal meaning and sometimes they don't, but an understanding of the meaning is never the point. That is why most translations of this sutra, whether into Chinese, Tibetan, Japanese, Korean, French, or English, leave the mantra in the original Sanskrit. These words do, nonetheless, have a meaning. *Gate* means "gone." *Paragate* is something like "gone beyond" or "gone over to the other shore," which harkens back to the metaphor the Buddha often used for enlightenment as crossing the river of suffering and samsara to the shore of liberation. *Parasamgate* means "gone completely beyond." The term *bodhi* is, of course, closely related to *buddha*, and means enlightenment, while *svaha* is a cry of joy or excitement often used at the end of Vedic rituals, something like "hurrah!" or "may it be so!" So altogether we have "Gone, gone, gone beyond, gone completely beyond, enlightenment!" This is why the full title of this sutra is sometimes given as the *Wisdom Beyond Wisdom Heart Sutra.* Wisdom beyond understanding. Wisdom beyond thought. Wisdom beyond wisdom. Gone, gone, gone beyond the suffering of samsara, gone beyond the bliss of nirvana, gone completely beyond absolutely everything, hail enlightenment!

The Empty Path

Those who approach these teachings from a purely intellectual standpoint may find it strange that these sutras warn us their own teachings are terrifying and describe the violent, even fatal, reactions of many of the monks. But if we go beyond the intellectual level to the depths of these teachings, they not only reveal a tremendous power, but also a tremendous danger. For what happens once we have seen completely through everything we thought and believed? For those who are ripe, the answer is complete total liberation. But for others, it can be a terrifying experience or lead to grave misunderstandings. If one sees the emptiness

of conventional moral standards and beliefs before they are truly liberated from their greed, hate, and delusion, the results can be disastrous.
The American Zen master Tenshin Reb Anderson bluntly recognizes
this danger and tells his students that if practicing the prajnaparamita
makes you think the ethical precepts don't apply to you, then it is time
to try another practice.

But there is another kind of problem as well, and much of the history of Mahayana Buddhism can be seen as the story of the way different
traditions responded to it. If the four noble truths, the eightfold path,
and all the logical systematic practices of the first turning are just empty
words, what then of our practice and our need for guidance? If the great
realization of emptiness doesn't spontaneously dawn on us, what do we
do then?

One path out of this dead end is offered by the meditation practices that seek to bypass the conceptual mind with all its notions of
goals, achievement, and spiritual progress. The mantra offered by the
Heart Sutra points the way to such an escape route: tantric practices
that invoke the power of ritual and imagination to speak to deeper levels
of cognition below the rational mind. These practices usually start with
an introductory ritual that involves chanting, visualizations, and perhaps
some specific ritualized actions. Then the practitioner begins repeating the mantra and visualizing the *yidam,* the enlightened being, that
is associated with it. These visualizations can be very demanding and
certainly serve to heighten the intensity of the practitioner's concentration, but they do much more than that. They are rooted in a deep ritual
and symbolic context, and they seek to plant the seed of enlightenment
in the deepest levels of the subconscious mind. The yidam embodies
one or more of the enlightened powers of the mind, and the rituals and
visualizations seek to bring the practitioner into the sacred mandala of
that being.

Although Avalokiteshvara never mentions his own mantra, *Om mani
padmi hum,* in the *Heart Sutra,* it is the most well-known and widely
chanted of all the tantric mantras and is an excellent example of how
mantra practice works. A typical practitioner might begin a session by
chanting a preliminary text, and then repeat the mantra over and over

again while visualizing Avalokiteshvara above her head, adorned with resplendent jewels while his arms, which in some visualizations may run into the thousands, hold various ritual objects. Avalokiteshvara symbolizes pure compassion, but he is more than that. He is compassion personified—compassion with a human face and human body. As the practitioner evokes the image of Avalokiteshvara, she evokes the boundless compassion of the enlightened beings, and eventually she actually becomes the yidam and actualizes that boundless compassion within herself.

In the same way, the mantra offered in the *Heart Sutra* (*Gate, gate, paragate, parasamgate, bodhi svaha*) is the mantra of the great Prajnaparamita, the mother of all buddhas, but instead of compassion she is the personification of emptiness—the wisdom beyond wisdom.

The great Zen masters of ancient China didn't follow the tantric path pioneered in India and Tibet, but developed their own unique response to this "crisis of emptiness." Their approach was more a frontal assault on the thinking mind than an end run around it. From its very beginnings, Zen was steeped in the emptiness teachings of the Perfection of Wisdom. But during the Tang Dynasty, great masters like Mazu and Linji developed a host of new techniques to break their students' attachment to their habitual patterns of thought with a sudden shattering blow. Sometimes it was a completely unexpected answer to a student's question, an ear-splitting shout, or even a physical assault. One favored device was to ask a student an unanswerable question and then to shout suddenly in his ear while he was struggling for an answer. Mazu's students were likely to be pummeled with blows at the most unexpected moments, and he is even credited with enlightening one monk by painfully twisting his nose. This famous proclamation by Linji is clearly very much in the spirit of the *Heart Sutra*:

> Followers of the Way, if you want insight into dharma as it is, just don't be taken in by the deluded views of others. Whatever you encounter, either within or without, slay it at once: on meeting a buddha slay the buddha, on meeting a patriarch slay the patriarch, on meeting an arhat slay the arhat, on meeting your parents slay your

parents, on meeting your kinsman slay your kinsman, and you attain emancipation. By not cleaving to things, you freely pass through.[42]

Eventually these radical techniques were systematized in the study of koans or "public cases," which were sometimes based on stories about the great masters of the Tang era. These koans typically pose a question or riddle whose solution lies beyond the reach of the rational mind: "Show me your face before your parents were born." "You know the sound of two hand clapping, what is the sound of one hand clapping?" Monks are usually assigned a particular koan and expected to work on it in their meditation and throughout their day. They are forced to demonstrate their understanding in regularly scheduled interviews with their teacher, who might respond with everything from warm praise to a blow on the head.[43] The rational calculating mind was of no use here, for the student might find that the same answer the master greeted with a blow or an angry shout when he first began working on the koan elicited loving congratulations when his mind was ripe. After being judged to have "passed" a koan, the student is given another more difficult one, until he has completed the course of study.

Finally, there is the path of meditation without structure or goal that some call formless meditation. Known as *shikantaza* (just sitting) in the Soto school of Japanese Zen and "nonmeditation" in the Mahamudra practice of Tibet's Kagyu sect, this path is also an essential part of Dzogchen practice among the Nyingmas of Tibet. The technique, if it can be called that, is the essence of simplicity. The meditator simply sits down and pays attention. There are really no rules, no further instructions, and no goal. Many consider this the highest form of meditation, but it is obviously an extremely difficult practice, since it can easily slide into mere drowsiness or daydreaming, and for that reason it is often given to only the most advanced students. Mahamudra meditators, for example, typically begin practice of "nonmeditation" only after years of preliminary practices have laid the foundation.

But if Avalokiteshvara is right and there is no goal and absolutely nothing to achieve, why meditate at all? Eihei Dogen, the great founder of Soto Zen in Japan, answered this profound question in no uncertain terms. We do not practice meditation *in order to* become enlightened. We practice meditation *because* we are enlightened. Meditation is the natural expression of our deepest true nature manifesting in this world.

Two Truths

The struggle over how to resolve the apparent contradiction between the teachings of the first and the second turnings of the wheel has been a central issue of Buddhist thought for the last two thousand years, and it remains a burning question in the twenty-first century. Of course, some simply reject one set of teachings and follow the other. But if we look at all the great masters who have come from both traditions, it seems untenable to hold one as true and the other false. The third turning of the wheel was part of a very explicit attempt to resolve this problem, but before we examine it, we need to consider another popular solution: the idea that these two types of teachings represent two more or less separate kinds of truth.

The notion that there is an absolute and a relative truth was central to the work of the great philosopher Nagarjuna, and it became particularly important to the monks of the Geluk sect of Tibetan Buddhism who came to see it as a key to understanding all the divergent Buddhist paths.[44] A less philosophical version of this theory of two truths has become popular among a broad range of contemporary Buddhists.

The general idea is that there is an absolute truth that is emptiness or an ultimate oneness, as well as the relative truth of our everyday lives in samsara. Those who stick most closely to the traditional interpretation hold that when we look with the eyes of wisdom we see the absolute truth, and when looking with the eyes of delusion we see the relative truth. But if this relative truth is only a product of our delusion, why call it truth at all? The Tibetan scholar Khenpo Tsultrim Gyamtso, who has been extensively involved with the effort to translate such traditional terms into English, prefers to call these two visions of reality "apparent truth" and "genuine truth," and I think that translation makes things much more clear. But it's still important to recognize that apparent truth still has some kind of reality—the reality of insubstantial appearances that come and go.

Many contemporary Buddhists, however, conceive of the two truths as relatively coequal perspectives on reality. When looking from the absolute perspective, one sees emptiness, and when looking from the relative perspective, one sees the vast diversity of interdependent things. These two views are like two sides of the same coin, both true from their own perspective. An appeal to these two truths is probably the most popular way that contemporary Western Buddhists resolve the contradictions between the teachings of the first and the second turnings. The four noble truths, the eightfold path, the precepts, and most of the other teachings of the first turning are relative truth, while the emptiness teachings of the second turning are absolute truth. Both are held to be true from their own perspective.

The doctrine of the two truths is subtle and hard to grasp, and either approach to understanding it has dangers. If we see the relative truth as the mere product of our delusion, we run the risk of neglecting our everyday lives and their difficulties in what is sometimes called a "spiritual bypass." But if we see the two truths as two coequal spheres, we may open a back door that allows us to continue to cling to our dreams and delusions as some kind of "relative truth." If the *Heart Sutra* had addressed this issue, I suspect it would have told us in no uncertain terms that there is no relative truth and no absolute truth.

As important as it is, moreover, an understanding of the two truths still does not resolve the practical side of the problem: What should a Buddhist practitioner do when confronted, on the one hand, with the systematic step-by-step program to attain nirvana laid out in the first turning of the wheel, and, on the other, with the goal-less nonattainment of the second turning? It is in search of answers to this dilemma that we now move to explore the third turning of the wheel.

3

The Third Turning of the Wheel: Awakened Nature and Everyday Consciousness

The third turning of the wheel was set in motion by the towering *Sutra of the Explanation of the Profound Secrets* (*Samdhinirmocana Sutra*), and it will be our starting point and our touchstone. Few Westerners, or for that matter few Asians, have even heard this sutra, much less tried to read it, but its depth of insight, its psychological sophistication, and its logical systematic presentation give it a natural appeal in our twenty-first-century world. Its tongue-twisting Sanskrit title lends itself to many different translations including "Untying the Knot," "Sutra that Explains the Profound Secret," "Explanation of the Mysteries," and "Sutra Explaining the Buddha's Thought."[45] As you might be able to tell from these titles, one of the central themes of this sutra, which runs to over a hundred pages in its English translations, speaks directly to the issue we brought up at the end of the last chapter: why does the Buddha give such radically different teachings in the first and second turnings of the wheel? Was there some underlying meaning he was trying to get across, and if so, what does it tell us about our lives and our practice?

At the very beginning of the sutra, the Buddha tells us that however different they may appear on the surface, the underlying meaning of his teachings is "all of one taste." As we have seen, the first turning of the wheel gave us a logical, systematic understanding of the path and its goal, while the second turning dismantled all such understanding and pointed directly to the ultimate truth beyond all words. The third turning, beginning with the *Sutra of the Explanation of the Profound Secrets*, reintroduced a logical systematic understanding of the path— but one based on the realization that in truth there is no logical systematic understanding and no path. If this seems completely confusing, bear with me and I think it will become more clear as we go along.

Reality Is Ungraspable

The *Sutra of the Explanation of the Profound Secrets* opens with an image of the Buddha sitting in a wondrous palace surrounded by a vast retinue. Legions of bodhisattvas and other great beings have gathered there "like clouds" to hear his teachings. The Buddha himself is perfectly absorbed in the "teachings of signlessness" and he "abides the way a buddha abides."

The sutra is structured around a series of questions put to the Buddha (or in one case to his stand-in, the Bodhisattva Gambhirarthasamdhinirmocana, whose jawbreaking name means "Unlocking the Implicit Intent of the Profound Doctrine"). The very first questions seek to clarify the puzzling logic the Buddha used in the second turning. Not surprisingly, the questioner, Bodhisattva Vidhivatpariprcchaka ("Logical Questioner"), is taken aback when he is told that ". . . all things are of two kinds, conditioned and unconditioned [or created and uncreated]. Herein conditioned things are neither conditioned nor unconditioned, and unconditioned things are neither unconditioned nor conditioned."[46] When he asks for an explanation of this puzzling statement, he receives an even more startling response: conditioned and unconditioned are just "provisional word[s] invented by the Buddha," and they, like all other words, "do not validate a real thing."[47] These passages are a translation of a translation of a very ancient text (the original Sanskrit has been lost), so it is not surprising that the wording seems a little awkward to contemporary ears. To put it simply, it is saying that words are nothing more than social inventions. They are not real and neither are the meanings they convey. What most people see as reality is actually nothing but a product of the imagination.

It is easy to misunderstand such statements, and it is important not to confuse them with some kind of world-denying nihilism. Bodhisattva Gambhirarthasamdhinirmocana explicitly tells us that the reality being discussed in these teachings is a "reality apart from language and realized in the perfect awakening of the saints through their holy wisdom and insight apart from all names and words."[48] Clearly, the point then is not that nothing is real, but that reality cannot be captured in our words and concepts.

But if reality is a signless realm beyond all words and conceptual thought, why do the awakened ones use words and concepts at all? The answer is obvious. According to the sutra, it is "because they desire to lead others to realize perfect awakening."[49] The words and the teachings are intended only to guide others to liberation, but some who suffer in ignorance cling to those words as if they were truly expressing reality.

So there it is. The truth underlying all those specific instructions from the first turning and all the paradoxical teachings from the second turning is explicitly spelled out. The reality of the ultimate simply cannot be put into words: "ultimate truth transcends all objects of thought and deliberation."[50] All the teachings are just provisional attempts to point us along the way.

There is a beautiful metaphor in another sutra of the third turning, the *Lankavatara*: The teachings are like a finger pointing at the moon of enlightenment. But people become attached to the finger, and "because they never look away from it, they are never able to discover the true meaning beyond the finger of words."[51] In another part of that same sutra the Buddha tells us, "nothing I reveal is real":

Thus, my teachings are diverse
tailored to the situation
if a teaching doesn't fit
then it isn't taught

Because each patient differs,
good physicians adjust their cures
buddhas thus teach beings
according to their capacities.[52]

There are passages in the early sutras in which the Buddha gives someone who is ready teachings from the second and third turnings.[53] But there was definitely a historical progression from one turning to the next. Why not just start off giving the highest teachings to everyone? As the American Zen Master Tenshin Reb Anderson points out, the Buddha faced two serious problems. For one thing, if he had started off by publicly proclaiming that he had nothing to teach because no words can capture the truth, a lot of people would probably have thought, "Well if that's true, why should I bother to listen to him?" But an even greater danger was that some people would see that the precepts and ethical rules were empty before they had liberated themselves from the greed, hate, and delusion they were intended to release. By the time the teachings of the second turning of the wheel began to spread some four hundred years after the Buddha's death, things had radically changed. Generations of students had been following the precepts and practicing the noble eightfold path, and many had directly tasted the truth of the Buddha's words or at least knew others who had, so the original danger that his teachings would simply be ignored was greatly reduced. But on the other hand, the Buddha's very success increased the danger that his followers would become attached and cling to his teachings. The second turning of the wheel attacked this problem head on. But as we have seen, by pulling the rug out from under the old teachings, it left some people rudderless and lacking the guidance they needed. So the teachings of the third turning came to the fore to provide the detailed conceptual instructions many people needed, while still making it clear that the truth realized by buddhas transcends any teachings.

Having driven home the point that the ultimate is beyond all words and concepts, the *Sutra of the Explanation of the Profound Secrets* offers us some more words to point us in the right direction—within ourselves. "Ultimate meaning is realized internally by each saint, while reasoning is attained in the give and take (of joint discussion) among common worldlings."[54] From the descriptions that have come down to us in the sutras, the monasteries of third-century India must have been full of scholastic monks reasoning and arguing about the fine points of Buddhist doctrine. But in the *Sutra of the Explanation of the Profound Secrets* the Buddha makes it crystal clear that the ultimate truth "stops all argument, transcends all aspects of thought and deliberation."[55] The Buddha makes this point again in the next chapter of the sutra, when the Bodhisattva Suvisuddhamati ("Purified Intelligence") tells him about a place he has been where he saw many bodhisattvas arguing about whether the ultimate and the conditioned were the same or different. The Buddha tells him: "The realm of actions and ultimate truth are beyond sameness and difference. Those who discriminate sameness and difference are not acting rightly."[56]

It is, nonetheless, important to be clear that even though he recognized the limits of logical thought, especially when applied to the ultimate, the Buddha never rejected logic itself. In fact, the Buddha often made logical arguments in the sutras, if that was what was needed to help his listeners wake up. What he rejected was argumentation driven by pride and conceit. Later in the sutra the Buddha's venerable disciple Subhuti makes this point when he tells the Buddha a story of a forest hermitage in which he once lived. The monks there argued endlessly about their views and understandings of various Buddhist doctrines. Subhuti says, "All of them cherished their pride, and because they clung to that pride, they were unable to comprehend the one universal taste of the truth of ultimate meaning."[57] We don't need to leave our logical minds at the door of liberation. What we do need to leave behind is our arrogance, and the belief that only we hold the truth.

The Psychological Dimension

In the next chapter, the Buddha makes a sharp pivot and turns to examine the psychological foundations of experience. The earlier chapters of the sutra are far too explicit about the limits of words and concepts for us to take these teachings as anything but a kind of useful fiction. But like all the Buddha's teachings, they are a fiction intended to help liberate us from our delusions, and that indeed they do.

Although the *Sutra of the Explanation of the Profound Secrets*'s primary psychological presentation is only about four pages long, it adds a new subconscious dimension that helps reorient our entire understanding of the psychological dynamics of delusion and awakening. The chapter begins when Visalamati (whose name means "Vast Intelligence") asks the Buddha the following question:

> . . . how are bodhisattvas wise with respect to the secrets of mind, thought, and consciousness? For what reason does the Tathagata designate a bodhisattva as wise with respect to the secrets of mind, thought, and consciousness?[58]

As he usually does, the Buddha first compliments his questioner for his good intentions and then sets out to answer his question. And it is a surprising answer indeed.

The Buddha tells Visalamati that no matter how beings are born into this world, from the very first instant, ". . . the mind which has all the seeds ripens; it develops, increases, and expands in its operation."[59] This "mind which has all the seeds" is the part of the mind beneath our usual conscious awareness that contains all the potentials, predisposition, and propensities that make us what were are. The development of this mind depends on two types of these "seeds." One is the predisposition to attach itself to a body with its sense powers. Thus this form of consciousness provides the physical body's animating life force. The other predisposition is toward dualistic thinking and the proliferation of images and concepts that for humans gives birth to the symbolic world in which we live.

The Buddha tells Visalamati that this consciousness is also called the "appropriating consciousness" because it takes possession or appropriates a body and its senses, and "repository consciousness" or "mind" because it stores the impressions of material forms, sounds, odors, tastes, and touch. So the *alaya vijnana,* as it is usually known in Sanskrit, is a kind of storehouse. On the one hand, it has those two kinds of universal predispositions that shape our behavior and development. On the other, it is the repository for the seeds or traces left by the individual's behavior and experience. And like seeds, the karmic results of our actions that are stored in the alaya vijnana eventually ripen to produce their fruit—be it good or bad.

These few short sentences amount to nothing less than a psychological revolution, for they announced the discovery of the subconscious mind some seventeen centuries before Freud. To understand their importance, we have to go back once again to the Abhidharma—the effort by Buddhist monks to organize the teachings of the first turning into a systematic whole that Edward Conze describes as the "world's first recorded psychology."[60] In this tradition, human experience is nothing more than a rapid succession of momentary experiences, each one dependent upon and shaped by its predecessor. There is no other underlying unity to this process. Each of us is simply a "mind stream" of cascading events that in our delusion we take to be some kind of independent self. But as useful as this theory is, it soon ran up against some serious explanatory problems.

One of the highest attainments for monks in the early schools of Buddhism was a state known as *nirodha* or cessation. In this state, which according to traditional sources might last as long as a week, all thought and perception cease, and the mind became something of a blank slate. Abhidharma theory clearly implies that such a cessation of mental activity would have to be permanent. Since the chain of succeeding mental events had been broken, there would be no cause for new mental events to occur. But, of course, monks did in fact spontaneously emerge from this cessation and return to everyday reality.[61]

The solution offered in this sutra is that there is something that continues in the state of cessation after conscious awareness has ended: the alaya vijnana. The existence of this storehouse also helps explain a number of other mysteries, such as how the karmic results of someone's actions might not appear until years or even decades later and exactly what it is that continues on from one lifetime to another. But more importantly, this concept gives us a powerful new way to understand the path to awakening and the problems people encounter while on it.

After that initial description, the Buddha goes on to tell us that as this appropriating consciousness develops:

> the sixfold collections of consciousness—the eye consciousness,
> ear consciousness, nose consciousness, tongue consciousness, body
> consciousness, and mind consciousness—arise depending upon

and abiding in that appropriating consciousness. An eye consciousness arises depending on an eye and a form in association with
consciousness. Functioning together with that eye consciousness a
conceptual mental consciousness arises at the same time, having
the same objective reference.[62]

Most of this passage is a brief restatement of the Abhidharma's theory
of perception that we first met in the previous chapter, but there is one
critical addition. In the Abhidharma, whenever there is a conjunction
of a sense organ and an object, a sense consciousness arises. As soon as
one of these five sense consciousnesses arises, a "mind consciousness"
takes it as its object and creates a mental image based on the original
sense consciousness. So we are seldom actually aware of our direct sense
perceptions, but only of the image our mind creates of them, and thus
most of the time our perception of the world is fundamentally distorted.
But in addition to those six consciousnesses found in the Abhidharma,
the *Sutra of the Explanation of the Profound Secrets* adds another—the
alaya vijnana that we just discussed—that underlies and supports all
the others. The distortions in the perception of the mind consciousness
actually arise from the deeply rooted predispositions of the alaya. Our
most fundamental delusion—that the world is made up of separate discrete objects that are being perceived by some independent observer,
some kind of self—is a direct projection of the its predisposition toward
dualistic thinking.

The relationship between the alaya vijnana and the other consciousnesses is, however, subtler and more complex than that statement would
make it seem. The alaya not only shapes our perceptions and experience,
but it is shaped by them as well. As the *Lankavatara Sutra* puts it:

Just like waves in a boundless sea
blown by a powerful wind
breakers in a black expanse
they never for a moment cease

In the Ocean of Alaya

stirred by the wind of externality
wave after wave of consciousness
breaks and swells again[63]

But as fascinating as the Buddha's story about the alaya vijnana is, it is a complete misunderstanding to see it as an attempt by ancient psychologists to arrive at a conceptual understanding of the mind and its operation. Like all the Buddha's teachings, it is intended only as a guide to help us on the path of liberation, and as such it is as relevant today as it was in the third century. Take for example the experience meditators sometimes have when the veil of delusion suddenly lifts and they have a profound opening to things just as they really are. Such experiences are so moving that it is common to feel one has been freed from suffering and delusion once and for all. Yet in a few days or weeks, all that suffering comes pouring back, leaving only puzzlement and confusion in its wake. The wisdom of the third turning provides us with the antidote to this confusion. It tells us that these openings in which our delusions and defilements seem to disappear are a wonderful part of the spiritual path, but if the seeds that gave them birth still remain in our subconscious, they will soon return. Final liberation does not come from any single experience, however profound, but only with the complete purification of the alaya.

This story of the alaya vijnana with all its seeds of delusion is, however, a controversial one, for like all such stories it is subject to deep misunderstandings. The greatest danger is that the alaya will be misconstrued as some kind of self—a danger so pronounced that some Buddhists reject any use of the term at all. I think that is throwing out the baby with the bathwater, but great care is needed lest we be led into further confusion. As the Buddha tells Visalamati at the end of their dialogue:

The appropriating consciousness is profound and subtle indeed,
all its seeds are like a rushing torrent.
Fearing that they would imagine and cling to it as to a self,
I have not revealed it to the foolish.[64]

The Three Characteristics of Phenomena

In response to the questions of Bodhisattva Gunakara, whose name means "Root of Virtue" in Sanskrit, the Buddha turns from the nature of mind to the nature of all things: that is, to the fundamental characteristics of phenomena. Gunakara asks the Buddha, "When you say 'Bodhisattvas are wise with respect to the character of phenomena.' . . . How are Bodhisattvas wise with respect to the character of phenomena?"[65] Once again the Buddha praises his questioner's good intentions and then goes on to tell Gunakara that there are actually three characteristics of phenomena: the imputational character, the other-dependent character, and the character of full perfection.[66] The Buddha starts by defining the imputational character.

> The pattern of clinging to what is entirely imagined [the imputational character] refers to the establishing of names and symbols for all things and the distinguishing of their essences, whereby they come to be expressed in language.[67]

In other words, one of the basic characteristics of all phenomena is that we imagine them to be something they are not. How can that be? Because of two predispositions deeply rooted in the alaya vijnana. First comes the predisposition to see the world as a collection of discrete independent things each with their own individual characteristics. And following quickly upon that is our predisposition to attach names and symbols to those independent things we imagine to exist, so we can make them an object of our thought and talk about them with others. At first this may sound like nothing but a kind of interesting academic point, but if you really understand what this passage is talking about, it is a revelation that threatens the whole foundation of your everyday "reality." All the ideas and beliefs we have about the world, even the discrete independent things we seem to see all around us, are nothing but pure imagination— just projections of our mind.

This is obviously a radical thing to say to in materialistic Western culture. Most of us would probably grant that our perceptions of the world are created by our minds. Even the most materialistic scientists would tell us that there is no blue or green in the physical world, only different wavelengths of light. But don't those constructions of our mind have to be based on something real and objective? In order to understand the Buddha's answer to this question, we need to examine the other two characteristics of phenomena.

In the next passage, the Buddha tells Gunakara that the other-dependent character of phenomena "is simply the dependent origination of phenomena. It is like this: Because this exists, that arises; because this is produced, that is produced."[68] This description of dependent origination comes straight from the first turning, and it is one of the fundamental principles of all traditions of Buddhism. It is, moreover, hardly a controversial idea. In fact, it seems to be just common sense. Things don't just pop into existence out of nowhere; they are caused by other things, which in turn have their own causes and on and on in an infinite web. But the implications of this simple truth are staggering. If every thing is dependent on something else, then every thing is unstable and impermanent. As soon as those supporting conditions change, the thing itself either changes or ceases to exist. Ours is a world of constant change in which nothing can be depended upon to stay the same: no seemly solid objects, no friends or loved ones, not even ourselves. The tighter we hold on to those things, the more we suffer.

Finally, the Buddha completes his description of the nature of things by explaining the characteristic of full perfection:

> Gunakara, what is the thoroughly established [perfected] character of phenomena? It is the suchness of phenomena.[69]

But what does it mean to say that the ultimate, perfect nature of things is their suchness? The Sanskrit term used here, *tathata*, isn't exactly a household word in the West, nor is it an easy concept to translate or define. It is usually rendered into English as "suchness" or "thusness." It is more or less equivalent to the concept of emptiness used so often in the sutras of the second turning, but it has, I think, a slightly more positive twist. Rather than talking about the nature of the ultimate in terms of its emptiness (as the *Sutra of the Explanation of the Profound Secrets* itself often does), the concept of thusness points to its fullness. No words can touch this ultimate character of reality, but it shines in the brilliant clarity of being exactly what it is—exactly thus. This does not mean, however, that the ultimate isn't empty. Elsewhere in the sutra the characteristic of full perfection is defined as "the absence of the imputational character in the other-dependent character," in other words, as the emptiness of the other-dependent character of the imputations we project on it.

The Buddha gives us two metaphors to help us understand the surprising relationship between these three characteristics of phenomena. The first is an eye with cataracts or "cloudy vision." The imputational character with its words, symbols, and images resembles a malfunctioning eye, because it distorts what we see. The other-dependent character is like the optical illusions produced by the cataracts. A person with cataracts might see images such as hairs, flies, small particles, or patches of different color when there isn't really anything there. Finally, the character of full perfection is the clear, undistorted vision of someone without cataracts or cloudy vision.

The second metaphor is that of a very clear pure crystal. If you were to shine a blue light on it, it might appear to be a sapphire, or if you shined a red light on it you might take it to be a ruby. The blue or red light is the imputational character with its images and words that we project out into the world. Our belief in the illusory ruby or sapphire is like our mistaken belief that the ideas and images we project on the world are actually real. The fact that the clear crystal never had the character of a ruby or sapphire that we projected upon it is the character of full perfection.

In the teachings of the first turning, the other-dependence of things is presented as an accurate description of the way they really are. But here the Buddha is telling us that other-dependency is only the way things appear to be when we see them through the filter of our images, conceptual categories, and words. It is liberating to understand things as being other-dependent and impermanent, because it helps loosen our attachment to them. But it can't lead to complete liberation, because it isn't really true. In reality, there are no things, and therefore there are no causes and nothing to arise or cease.

The Buddha sums up the relationship between the three natures in these words:

> Gunakara, in dependence upon names that are connected with signs, the imputational character is known. In dependence upon strongly adhering to the other-dependent character as being the imputational character, the other-dependent character is known. In dependence upon absence of strong adherence to the other-dependent character as being the imputational character, the thoroughly established [perfected] character is known.[70]

The true nature of reality is inconceivable and ungraspable. It is a complete and total mystery. The only way we can know or talk about it is by confusing it with our words, concepts, and projections. But if we truly realize that reality is completely untouched by our projections, then we realize the full perfection of the world.

Notice, however, that the sutra doesn't say that we have to stop all the projections of our mind, only that we have to stop grasping and believing in them. Many spiritual seekers feel that liberation requires that we live in mental silence without any words or projections at all. While such a profound silence is a kind of liberation, it is personal liberation, not the great liberation of the bodhisattvas. To really benefit beings, the bodhisattva cannot stand on some distant mountaintop. She must enter the world of suffering beings with their words, concepts, and signs, and take on the chains of delusion so that one by one they may be broken.

Buddha Nature

After the second turning dissolved all appearance and all the teachings into pure emptiness, the Buddha turned the wheel of Dharma again to correct the profound misinterpretation many people had of those new teachings as a nihilistic denial of all existence. As we have seen, he painted a map of the psyche to help guide our practice, and he showed us exactly how we create our delusion and suffering by projecting out our dualistic patterns of thought onto the world. Finally, the Buddha gave us a more positive description of the ultimate to balance the misunderstanding some people had of emptiness from the second turning. Although this teaching is present only in the barest outlines in the *Sutra of the Explanation of the Profound Secrets*, it was spelled out in many other sutras such as the *Tathagatagarbha Sutra* and the *Lion's Roar of Queen Srimala*. Some fear that this more-positive characterization of the ultimate runs the risk of becoming an object of our deluded attachments, but it is widely accepted in most schools of Buddhism in Tibet and East Asia, and it provides a powerful antidote for the sense of negativity some people get from the emptiness teachings.

The sutras use a variety of Sanskrit names to refer to this ultimate, including the *tathatagarbha* and *dharmakaya*. The term most commonly used in English is "buddha nature," although there are lots of others. So what is this buddha nature? Obviously, we have to tread very lightly in answering this question, since as we have seen, words are not capable of even capturing the reality of the everyday world, much less of the ultimate nature of things.

The *Tathagatagarbha Sutra* avoids giving us a concrete description of our awakened buddha nature and instead relies on implication and example. First off, the Buddha tells us that when he looks beneath the greed, hatred, confusion, and obscuration of suffering beings, he sees that they "have a tathagata-garbha that is eternally unsullied, and that is replete with virtues no different from my own."[71] Then he goes on to give us a series of poetic similes. First, the tathatagarbha is likened to honey surrounded by a swarm of angry bees:

> All beings have the Tathagata-garbha. It is like pure honey in a cave or tree, but it is covered by kleshas [defilements], which, like a swarm of bees, keep one from getting to it. With my Buddha eye I see it clearly, and with appropriate virtuous expedients I expound the Dharma, in order to destroy kleshas and reveal the Buddha vision.

It is a nugget of gold that fell into a cesspool many years ago:

The pure gold does not decay, yet no one knows that it is there. But suppose there came along someone with supernatural vision, who told people, "Within the impure waste there is a genuine gold trinket. You should get it out and do with it as you please." Similarly, kulaputras, the impure waste is your innumerable kleshas. The genuine gold trinket is your tathagatagarbha. For this reason, the Tathagata widely expounds the Dharma to enable all beings to destroy their kleshas, attain correct perfect enlightment and perform Buddha deeds.

It is a statue of pure gold that is still covered by the mold that was used to cast it:

After casting is complete, it is inverted and placed on the ground. Although the outside is scorched and blackened, the inside is unchanged. When it is opened and the statue taken out, the golden color is radiant and dazzling. Similarly, kulaputras, when the Tathagata observes all beings, he sees that the Buddhagarbha is inside their bodies replete with all its many virtues. After seeing this, he reveals far and wide that all beings will obtain relief. He removes kleshas with his Vajrajnana (diamond wisdom) and reveals the Buddha-kaya like a person uncovering a golden statue.

In the *Lion's Roar of Queen Srimala,* the wise queen gives the approving Buddha a more concrete description of the dharmakaya. It has "indestructible, eternal, unchanging, and inconceivable merits,"[72] and the dharmakaya "is the perfection of permanence, the perfection of happiness, the perfection of the substantial self, and the perfection of purity."[73]

In the Tibetan tradition, our buddha nature is often described as luminous emptiness. Although essentially empty, it has the illuminating potential to know and experience. Queen Srimala also tells us that the tathagatagarbha is "the basis, support, and foundation of conditioned phenomena."[74] It is, in other words, the ultimate from which all else arises.

The *Lankavatara* helps complete the great psychological system presented in the teachings of the third turning by grounding it in tathagatagarbha. In it, the Buddha explains how the various consciousnesses we discussed earlier arise from tathagatagarbha when it is "impregnated" by the seeds of delusion:

> The tathagata-garbha is the cause of whatever is good or bad and is responsible for every form of existence everywhere . . . When it is impregnated by the habit-energy of beginningless fabrications, it is known as the repository consciousness (alaya) and gives birth to fundamental ignorance along with seven kinds of consciousness. It is like the ocean whose waves arise without cease. But it transcends the misconception of impermanence or the conceit of a self and is essentially pure and clear.[75]

Everything arises from this ungraspable, undefinable ultimate. It is our deepest true nature, but we become confused by the vast array of appearances our habit energy stirs up and lose sight of what we truly are.

Perhaps the most comprehensive attempt to describe this indescribable buddha nature comes not from the sutras but a shastra (commentary on the sutras), albeit one so revered that is held to be the work of Maitreya, the Buddha to come. Maitreya tells us that buddha nature is "uncreated and spontaneously present, not a realization due to extraneous conditions, wielding knowledge, compassionate love, and ability."[76] Thus, the buddha nature at the core of our being spontaneously manifests wisdom, love, and power that can cut through all our suffering and delusions if we allow it to.

Practicing the Third Turning

In the first turning of the wheel, the Buddha set out a clear step-by-step road to liberation. As we have seen, the first step is when one hears the teachings and is inspired to follow the path of renunciation. The Buddha encouraged his followers, both with his words and by his example, to became monks and give up the ties that bound them to samsara. A monk lived by the strictest moral discipline, renounced sex, marriage, and the other pleasures of family life, ate only a single meal a day, and lived the most austere of lifestyles begging for the food that sustained him. He dedicated himself to the practice of mindfulness and concentration, and step by step progressed down the path until he reached nirvana and was freed once and for all from rebirth into the world of samara.

The teachings of the second turning completely dismantled this whole system. There is no path, no suffering, and no end of suffering. There is no attainment because everyone is free from the start. The idea of achieving nirvana is therefore only a delusion. Nirvana and samara are not really different or the same, and one cannot reach them because they are always present at all times. Practice becomes more an expression of our true enlightened nature than a way of achieving anything.

The third turning of the wheel reestablished a systematic conceptual path to liberation that has much in common with the path outlined in the first turning, but its underlying assumptions had profoundly shifted. Rather than the holy truth the followers of the first turning often assumed it to be, this description of the path was just a useful story the Buddha told us out of his great compassion. The implications of this philosophical shift were subtle but profound and far-reaching. If, for example, samsara and nirvana aren't really different, then the whole idea of renouncing samsara and striving to attain nirvana really doesn't make much sense.

But what then of the monastic ideal? The answer to that question is a complex one, for the monks and the monasteries remained Buddhism's most central social institution throughout its long history in Asia. Nonetheless, the Mahayana teachings clearly signaled the growth of a competing ideal. The picture the *Sutra of the Explanation of the Profound Secrets* paints of the monks is, for example, hardly a flattering one. The monks described in the sutra are vain, prideful, and engaged in constant intellectual bickering based on their own conceited views. The Mahayana sutras are more likely to recommend that seekers go to live in the forests or mountains than in the monasteries.[77] In other sutras, laymen like Vimalakirti surpass the monks in their understanding, and for the first time women such as Queen Srimala teach the Dharma.

Although the path of worldly renunciation is given great respect in these sutras, it is clearly held to be inferior to that of the bodhisattva who remains in the midst of the suffering of the world. In the *Sutra of the Explanation of the Profound Secrets*, as in many of the other Mahayana sutras, the Buddha says in no uncertain terms that those who aim only for the great peace of the arhat will never be able to attain unsurpassed perfect enlightenment:

> Since their compassion has been weak, they have turned their backs upon deeds that benefit and gladden all sentient beings. Since they have lived in fear of suffering they have turned their backs upon engendering any conditioned activities.[78] I do not describe those who turn away from the welfare of sentient beings and who turn away from all the activities of compounded existence as unsurpassably, perfectly enlightened.[79]

Another contrast, although a much smaller one, is the way the two approach the ethical foundations of practice. Like most ethical systems, Buddhism has both things you should do (practice the perfections) and things you shouldn't do (violate the precepts). The ethics of the first turning emphasized the prohibitions laid out in the precepts. For laypeople there were only five—do not kill, lie, steal, misuse sexuality, or become intoxicated—but with ordination a monk took on hundreds more. The second and third turnings placed more emphasis on what are called *paramitas* in Sanskrit. This term can be translated as the perfections, those that go beyond, or transcendence. The most common list has six of these perfections, but four additional paramitas are often added that, according to the *Sutra of the Explanation of the Profound Secrets*, act as supports for the first six.[80]

Although the practice of each paramita reinforces the practice of all the others, *Sutra of the Explanation of the Profound Secrets* tells us that they follow in a progressive order. The practice of the first paramita provides the support necessary to practice the next paramita successfully, and so on down the line. The list starts with the paramita of generosity, and those who give selflessly of their resources and of themselves find it easy to practice the next paramita, ethical behavior, which is often described in terms of the precepts. With the practice of ethical behavior one becomes patient, which is the third paramita. The practice of patience in turn supports the development of the fourth paramita: diligence and zeal. And diligent effort is essential for the next paramita, meditative concentration. Finally, meditation leads the bodhisattva to the final perfection: prajnaparamita, or the perfection of wisdom, which is the heart and soul of the bodhisattva path.

We have already gone into prajnaparamita in the chapter on the second turning, and what it means to practice generosity, ethical behavior, patience, and diligence are, I think, fairly clear. But how should one practice the perfection of meditation? The clearest, most comprehensive meditation instructions to be found in the sutras of the second and third turnings are once again found in the *Sutra of the Explanation of the Profound Secrets*, but it takes a little digging to put them together. Because the sutra is structured around the questions different bodhisattvas put to the Buddha, it tends to jump around a lot. The first meditation instructions the Buddha gives are actually for more advanced practitioners, and the beginning stages are filled in later on.

This path begins when the seekers hear the Dharma and dedicate themselves to practicing generosity, ethical behavior, patience, and diligence, and finally they turn to meditation. Typical of its analytic approach, the *Sutra of the Explanation of the Profound Secrets* divides the styles of meditation into two broad categories—shamatha and vipassana—then gives instruction for how to practice them and how the two can eventually be combined.

What is the difference between shamatha and vipassana? In theory, shamatha focuses on the development of tranquility and vipassana on the development of wisdom or insight, but in practice the difference between the two is not always that clear. Indeed, even the great Maitreya, the buddha to come, wondered about it. In the *Sutra of the Explanation of the Profound Secrets* he asks the Buddha: "Bhagavan, are the path of shamatha and the path of vipassana different or not different?" The Buddha answers in typical Mahayana fashion that "although they are not different, they are also not the same."[81] He goes on to explain that they are the same in that they both involve focusing attention on the mind, but they are different because they focus on different objects. In shamatha one focuses on what the sutra calls the "the mind contemplated by any mind" or the "uninterrupted mind." In other words, the focus is on the tranquil mind uninterrupted by any thoughts or images. In vipassana, on the other hand, one uses conceptual images and thoughts—most particularly the teachings of the Dharma.

So the process works something like this. The bodhisattva goes to a secluded place, and settles herself inwardly. Then she focuses her attention on her empty mind—the mind without thoughts or images. This is similar to the jhana practice described in the many of the sutras, although the teachings of the first turning usually recommended more concrete objects of attention such as colored disks or the inward and outward flow of the breath. The fruit of this practice is a state of calm tranquility (shamatha) that is accompanied by physical and mental pliancy. The Buddha says that if you haven't achieved that of pliancy of mind, you aren't in a true state of shamatha.

Once the meditator is calm, flexible, and pliant, she pivots around and begins to contemplate the teachings. This is the practice of vipassana. But while any contemplation of the Dharma is beneficial, the sutra makes it very clear that true vipassana, like true shamatha, can only be done in that state of tranquil pliancy. So it is necessary to practice shamatha first, before one turns to vipassana.

The key difference in the vipassana of the first and third turnings is that the meditator contemplates different kinds of teachings. In the first turning, the focus is on such things as the four noble truths and the three marks of existence (impermanence, suffering, and nonself), while meditation on the three characteristics of phenomena is central to the new path laid out in the *Sutra of the Explanation of the Profound Secrets*. The contemplation of the other-dependent character of phenomena is the most basic of the three, and it is the foundation for meditation on the other two characters. In this practice, the meditator looks out at all the phenomena that arise in her mind and sees that they have not the slightest trace of independent existence, that they are wholly dependent on countless other causes and conditions. Every time something arises, she immediately recognizes that it is other-dependent, undependable, and impermanent. Over and over again she reminds herself that this phenomenon is other-dependent, this phenomenon is undependable, this phenomenon is impermanent, until it is like the beating of her heart. The Buddha tells us that as this meditation comes to fruition, we become less attached to this impermanent, undependable world of illusion, and that leads us to avoid wrongdoing and become more virtuous.

The meditation on the other-dependent nature of phenomena will not, however, lead us to final liberation, because the illusion that there are things and causes of those things still persists. So then we turn to the meditations on the imputational and perfected characteristics.

When meditating on the imputational character, we look to see exactly how those other-dependent objects appear as words and images. We see how we divide the seamless flux of the world up into little conceptual packages upon which we project the illusion of existence. When we see those projections for what they are—just projections—we see that they are completely unable to reach the reality of the world. As this process continues, we realize what a critical part of our everyday life those illusory words, signs, and concepts really are. Without them, we can't think about the world or share our thoughts with others. Those conceptual delusions are in a sense the price of admission to the world of human society. But that price is a heavy one, for it is easy to cling to our conceptual imputations, desperately seeking meaning and security in an imaginary world that can never provide them.

After we come to clearly recognize this process of imputation and its effects, we turn to look at the perfected nature of things—the complete and total absence of all the things we imagine and project upon the world in the way things really are. This is the ultimate object of observation for the purification of phenomena and the realization of their true nature.

The final step in this new meditation program is reached when the meditator combines shamatha and vipassana together and attends to the "one-pointed mind." What is the one-pointed mind? Maitreya asked the Buddha that exact question, and he replied: "It is the realization that: 'this image which is the focus of samadhi (whether it is conceptual or nonconceptual) is cognition-only. Having realized that, it is mental attention to suchness."[82]

The idea that all the phenomena we perceive are "mind only" or "appearance only" is the most famous part of this sutra, and it was an inspiration for a whole school of "idealist" Buddhist philosophy that rejected the very existence of the material world as anything separate from the mind. It would be fascinating to explore the subtle web of argumentation the great Buddhist philosophers have woven around this issue, but it would only be a distraction from our purpose here. The goal of this famous passage was not to make any kind of philosophical claim. It is about the process of meditation. It describes the profound realization that occurs when we see that the objects of mind we are focusing upon in our meditation and the mind that contemplates them are not two things but one. Everything rests in nondual unity—pure suchness. This is the realization that frees us from clinging to the deluded imaginings we project onto the world. This is the realization that finally frees us from all our suffering.

The mahamudra meditation of the Kagyu school of Tibetan Buddhism follows a very similar approach to the one outlined in the *Sutra of the Explanation of the Profound Secrets*. The student starts by developing tranquil pliancy with shamatha meditation, then shifts to the inquiry of vipassana and contemplates a series of challenging questions posed by the teacher. She might, for example, be told to let her mind rest in its own natural state and then be asked such questions as "What is the abiding nature of that mind?" "Does it have a shape or color?" "Does it have a boundary?" "Where does it comes from?" "Where does it go?" "What is the one who searches for that mind?" Finally, when the teacher decides she is ready, the student combines shamatha and vipassana in what is called "nonmeditation," in which all instructions are left behind and the student simply rests in the true awakened nature of her mind—what the *Sutra of the Explanation of the Profound Secrets* calls pure suchness.

Part II

Turning the Wheel
in the Twenty-First
Century

4

Living Dharma

If the great sutras are to be more than just modern-day museum pieces, we must make them our own. We have to do more than just translate them into new languages; we must forge a fresh understanding compatible with our own cultural perspectives—and then put that understanding into practice, on the meditation cushion and in our daily lives.

Just as the Chinese relied on their indigenous Taoist tradition to bring the Buddhist teachings into their cultural world, and the Tibetans used Bon Shamanism to do the same thing, Western science and particularly Western psychology are helping give birth to a Dharma truly at home in Western culture. Some fear the deepest meaning of the tradition will get lost in the transition, but that need not be so. The great sutras of the three turnings contain a profound psychological system that has a natural resonance with the deepest part of our Western approach. An understanding of this Buddhist psychology can be both a guide for our practice and a gateway to philosophical mysteries that lie beyond the bounds of psychology, and we will begin this chapter by trying to lay out its fundamental principles in a way that makes them clear and useful.

Intellectual understanding by itself is never enough, however. No matter how thoroughly we have studied the great sutras, bringing their timeless wisdom into our lives and our culture is no easy matter. Every individual is unique, and the needs and expectations of Western students can be far different from those in Buddhism's homeland. So next we will explore the ways the sutras can guide us in putting that intellectual understanding into practice in the midst of this chaotic postmodern world.

The View: The Psychology of the Sutras

Although it is scattered in bits and pieces in many different places, the great sutras contain a psychological system of unparalleled subtlety and sophistication. In fact, the Buddha was as much a psychologist as a philosopher or mystic. Although his psychology has much in common with our empirical Western psychology, the approach of the Buddha and his followers has one fundamental difference. Their most basic goal is not to understand the operations of the mind, but to liberate us from suffering. In a sense, our Western approach seeks to create an accurate map of our mental terrain, while the Buddhist seeks guidance to reach a place most of the empiricists don't even know exists—what the second and third turnings call "complete perfect enlightenment."

As we have seen, the first comprehensive Buddhist psychology was created by groups of monks as they attempted to organize the teachings the Buddha gave in the sutras of the first turning into a systematic whole. This massive endeavor, known as the Abhidharma, is sometimes called the "valley of dry bones" for its seemingly endless lists and classifications that attempt to categorize every possible moment of experience. From the modern Western standpoint, these categories can seem rather odd both for what they include as well as what they omit, but for the monks practicing in a traditional setting, the goal was nothing less than the classification and analysis of every possible experience they might have.

One can spend a lifetime studying the Abhidharma—many monks actually have—but the key point is that it is, as Edward Conze put it, a "method of accounting for our experiences, a method in which the 'I' and 'mine' are completely omitted."[83] To most of us, of course, nothing seems more certain than the basic fact of our own existence. A sense of *I*, *me*, and *mine* lies at the foundation of all our experience, and it may seem inconceivable that it is all just an illusion. Yet that is what the Buddha said from the time he first set the wheel of Dharma in motion.

When we really look for this self, it is nowhere to be found. Deep meditative inquiry reveals nothing but a series of passing momentary events with no separate entity, no self that experiences them. Just hearing such teachings is, of course, not enough to alter a lifetime of mental habits. But imagine for a moment what a great liberation it would be to let go of our rigid, fixated sense of self with all its constrictions and pain, and allow each moment to simply be as it is in its own natural purity.

In the teachings of the first turning, the Buddha broke all human experience up into five "heaps" (skandhas) of momentary experiences (dharmas), which quickly appear and pass away one after the other. To use the words of the great nineteenth-century American psychologist William James, we are nothing but a "stream of consciousness."[84] The Buddha himself described human experience with a very similar concept, *vinnanasota,* as well as *bhavasot*—a stream of being. Later Buddhist teachings often make reference to individual persons as a "mind stream" or a continuum. The metaphor of a river or stream implies something that is never fixed or still, but always flowing and changing, and there is certainly no teaching more central to all Buddhism than the impermanence of all phenomena and the reality of constant change that that implies.

The monastic scholars who compiled the Abhidharma went into great detail attempting to classify every possible dharma that might arise and describing how each one leads to the next in this rushing torrent of experience. As we have seen, however, the teachings of the second turning clearly moved away from the scholasticism of the Abhidharma; when the *Heart Sutra* presented its list of negations, it dissolved virtually all the basic tenants of the Abhidharma into pure emptiness. Those teachings were eventually brought back in the psychology of the third turning, although this time in the context of a much broader and more sophisticated understanding.

This new approach begins in the *Sutra of the Explanation of the Profound Secrets,* when the Buddha tells us that bodhisattvas are "wise with respect to the secrets of mind, thought, and consciousness."[85] In the chapter that follows, he both encourages our practice and lays out a road map of the psyche that adds new territory not covered in the teachings of the first turning. There is a brilliant simplicity in the Buddha's approach here; it tells us what we need to know but sticks to the basics, so there is less danger of becoming so intellectually involved that we lose sight of the real goal.

So what did the Buddha actually mean when he said that bodhisatt-vas are wise with respect to the secrets of mind, thought, and conscious-ness? The English translations usually used for the original Sanskrit terms aren't all that helpful. The English words "mind" and "consciousness," for instance, mean roughly the same thing, but they clearly signify some-thing quite different here. Unlike in many other sutras, "mind" refers to the *alaya vijnana* or storehouse consciousness: that is, the subconscious part of our psyche that provides the foundation for all awareness. In this passage, "consciousness" does not refer to all discriminating awareness as it sometimes does, but only to the five sense consciousnesses—eye, ear, nose, tongue, and body.[86] So a more descriptive English translation might be "the secrets of the subconscious mind, thought, and percep-tion," but of course, each of those new terms has its own shades of mean-ing that were not in the original.

More than an abstract psychological theory, these teachings provide us with a kind of road map to liberation. An understanding of the myster-ies of the subconscious reveals the seeds of delusion and awakening we all carry, and the ways we can cultivate those seeds and grow a garden of enlightened wisdom. The teachings on perception show us how our deluded view of the world comes into being and how we can come to see through it. An understanding of the thinking mind lays bare the way our dualistic thinking creates the sense of self and other, and allows us to slowly release our attachment to this fundamental source of our suffering.

The Hidden Depths

Why is it so terribly hard for us to see things the way they really are? Where do all these delusions come from, and why do they seem to domi-nate our thoughts and virtually all our perceptions? A key part of the answer is to be found in the subconscious tendencies and predispositions that lie hidden in the depths of our minds. We like to think of ourselves as autonomous independent actors, rationally evaluating our options, making choices, and consciously guiding our lives through all the difficulties presented by the world. Yet for most of us, our conscious awareness is really more like a tiny circle of light in a vast mysterious night. Much of what we do and perceive is dictated by powerful forces hiding in that darkness—forces we seldom recognize, much less understand.

The Abhidharma had no concept of the unconscious. It wasn't until the third turning of the wheel that Buddhist psychology recognized the importance of the unseen depths below our conscious awareness, but that was still long before the concept of the unconscious mind ever came into Western culture. As we have seen, the *Sutra of the Explanation of the Profound Secrets* calls this aspect of mind the *alaya vijnana*—a term that is frequently translated as "storehouse consciousness," "all-base consciousness" or "substrate consciousness," but etymologically it also carries the connotation of "clinging" or "attachment."[87] The sutra uses several other names for the unconscious as well; for instance, it is first mentioned simply as "the mind that has all the seeds."

The *Sutra of the Explanation of the Profound Secrets* never systematically describes this "mind that has all the seeds," but it does list a number of its basic characteristics that were later worked into a more complete picture. In its deepest nature, mind is pure undefiled suchness—uncreated, unending, and beyond all conceptualization—but in its manifestation as the alaya vijnana, it is also permeated by the seeds of delusion. The alaya provides the foundation for all the other aspects of mind and body. In one respect, it is the vivifying principle that brings energy to the body, something like the Chinese concept of *chi* or the Freudian id. But it goes far beyond these, for it is also the aspect of mind that continues from life to life and "appropriates a new body during the process of death and rebirth."[88] The alaya also provides the foundation for all other types of consciousness and therefore for all experience, and it is here that we get our deluded tendency to see the world in terms of self and other.

But the alaya vijnana is not just the basis of our experience, it is also a *result* of our experience. Our thoughts and actions lay down seeds that permeate the alaya and give us new tendencies for future thoughts and actions. Thus each individual's storehouse has both a unique individual character and a universal character that is shared with everyone else[89]—something like Carl Jung's idea of the collective unconscious. In this psychology, the operations of the psyche are based on a complex feedback loop in which the predispositions in the alaya engender various thoughts and actions, which in turn create new predispositions that reinforce or undermine the existing ones, and those in turn give rise to new patterns of action, which plant their own seeds, and on and on. So the alaya vijnana is not just a passive repository of seeds. Rather, in the words of the *Sutra of the Explanation of the Profound Secrets,* it "flows like a river." Even when its seeds are not manifested in our conscious mind, they are changing and interacting. They may come to fruition in response to a particular set of external circumstances, but they can also "ripen" spontaneously on their own.

This may all sound pretty abstract, but it is easy to see this process in our everyday lives. Any parent will tell you every child comes into this world with a different set of predispositions to think, act, and respond emotionally. Buddhists would attribute these differences to the presence of the seeds carried over from past lives and Western psychologists to individual genetic variations, but whatever the cause, the effect is the same. As children mature and gain some control over their actions, the choices they make reshape those predispositions, strengthening some and causing others to weaken. Contemporary psychological research has, for example, shown that "blowing off steam" with an angry outburst makes you more, not less, likely to get angry in the future. When you swear at that woman who cut you off at the signal, you plant the seeds for more anger; you will be more likely to yell at your daughter when she breaks your favorite plate or have a screaming fight with your spouse. On the other hand, if you respond to that fear and anger by trying to sympathize with the stress that drove the other driver to take such risks, you strengthen your seeds of compassion and understanding.

An understanding of the alaya vijnana can be a potent guide for our practice and our daily lives. The contemporary Buddhist teacher and scholar Thich Nhat Hanh uses the metaphor of a garden and its gardener to explain its operation:[90] The alaya vijnana is the garden and our thinking mind is its gardener. Our garden contains the seeds that we brought with us into this life, the ones that we planted, and the seeds that come from our culture as a whole. We "water" some seeds with our thoughts and actions, and they grow stronger. Other seeds are ignored, either intentionally or unintentionally, and they grow weaker. Moreover, these seeds actually interact with each other in the subconscious mind, so if we plant the seeds of wholesome qualities, they may eventually transform the unwholesome seeds and prevent them from ever growing into conscious manifestation. Thus, even small actions and passing thoughts are extremely important—they can nurture either the seeds of liberation or those of delusion. The challenge is to be good gardeners, to use our loving attention to grow a garden of enlightened wisdom.

Yet despite its explanatory power, the idea that our everyday mind is built on a deep unconscious foundation has been as controversial among Buddhists as it is in the West. The primary objection from other Buddhists is that the alaya vijnana comes too close to being some kind of independent self—something, of course, the Buddha specifically denied.[91] For their part, the Buddhists who founded this new psychological system were clearly aware of the danger of this kind of misinterpretation and the *Sutra of the Explanation of the Profound Secrets* explicitly warned against it from the start.[92]

The Process of Perception

It might seem that the way we perceive the world is just a matter of physiology, having little or nothing to do with the quest for liberation. But in the Buddhist perspective at least, what appears to us to be an objective view of the world is as much a product of our delusion as our sensory apparatus.

Part of the problem is that our minds are presented with a constant flood of sensations—more sounds, sights, tastes, and feelings than we can possibly hold in our awareness. William James called it an "undistinguishable, swarming *continuum* devoid of distinction or emphasis."[93] To make sense of it all, our perceptual process selects out tiny portions of those sensations, bundles them together, and attaches a concept to them: "chair," "book," "husband." From then on, we view the objects we have created as if they were separate independent things of which we are the detached observer. Every time we open our eyes or ears, we recreate this fundamental delusion of separation without ever realizing it.

The Abhidharma tells us that a sensation is created when three factors come together—a sense organ like an eye, a sense object, and a sense consciousness that is aware of the object. Then, in what contemporary psychology would call the process of perception, the mind consciousness forms an image of the original sense consciousness that is mixed with all kinds of feelings, preconceptions, assumptions, habits, and memories, as well as the impressions that arise from other senses operating at the same time. The final stage in the process of perception occurs when we attach a name and a concept to what were originally just raw sensations. As the *Sutra of the Explanation of the Profound Secrets* puts it, most people's "minds are permeated with language, their understanding follows upon language, their inclinations are toward language. Thus they cling to various imagined essences and characteristics."[94]

Once those sensations of color, shape, sound, taste, and bodily feelings become "Mom" or "a table" or "a slice of pizza," they are established as an independent thing that appears separate from our perceiving mind. But such labels are not just neutral descriptions; they are associated with a vast array of thoughts and beliefs that are automatically incorporated into the perception. The images our mind creates are also immediately mixed with the pleasant, unpleasant, or neutral feelings they set off. We see some objects as beautiful and others as frightening, repulsive, or just dull and unimportant, seldom stopping to realize that those qualities are not in the objects themselves but only in our mind. Traditional Buddhist psychology places great importance on this part of the perceptual process, because it is those feelings that lead to the grasping and aversion that produce suffering.

Every time an object of desire loses its attraction or fear turns into familiarity, we get a call to wake up and see what is really going on. Suppose, for example, that you see someone who looks like your mother crossing the street. The perception of your mother begins when certain sights and sounds stimulate your sensory awareness. A flood of feelings—happiness, surprise, or anger—arises as soon as she is identified, and perhaps the conversation you had with her that morning springs into your mind. You yell out a greeting, the woman turns, and she is a total stranger. Now those same sights and sounds that were your mother a second before become something else entirely.

We have all experienced this kind of perceptual disorientation that momentarily shakes us free from some of our preconceptions and assumptions. But the roots of our delusion run deep and are seldom called into question. Perhaps the deepest of all is our almost automatic tendency to see the world in dualistic terms. As soon as we see some kind of shape, perhaps associated with various sounds and tactile sensations, the mind transforms it into an independent thing and us into its observer. That table, that tree, that person over there are seen as external objects completely separate from our subjective personal awareness. This subject/object dualism blinds us to the reality of interdependence and our connection with all existence, and leads us into endless suffering.

The Thinking Mind

The thinking mind is the key to our liberation. It is the center of our conscious awareness, where our decisions to pursue wholesome or destructive actions are made. Moreover, according to the Tibetan master Khenchen Thrangu Rinpoche, "It is only the mind consciousness that can meditate."[95] When we practice tranquility meditation, it is the thinking consciousness that calms down. When we practice insight meditation, it is the thinking consciousness that experiences that insight. But let's be clear from the start; the kind of thinking we are talking about includes both thoughts and emotions.

In the West, of course, we tend to draw a sharp distinction between thoughts and emotions. Thought, especially reason and logic, is often seen as the unique human quality that sets us apart from the savagery of the "lower" animals. The emotions, on the other hand, are primitive and dangerous—a threat to the rational self-control that keeps us from succumbing to the ever-present temptations of sin and evil. Thus, we often go to war with ourselves, trying to repress the spontaneous manifestation of our natural feelings and to follow the dictates of a disembodied rationalism.

But are thoughts and emotions really two different things? Few would question the fact that some thoughts are inseparably linked to powerful emotions, but other thoughts seem far more neutral. In some cases, the pleasant or painful emotions associated with these thoughts are simply too weak for us to notice, but from the Buddhist standpoint even a neutral feeling is an emotion, just as much as strong feelings of joy or disgust. Viewed in this way, it is clear that even the most abstract thoughts carry an emotional charge.

But what about emotions that don't seem to be associated with any words or concepts? It is easy to dismiss such feelings as some kind of mindless physiological response, but the closer we look, the more it becomes clear that they have just as much meaning as more conceptual thoughts. Try this experiment the next time you feel some powerful emotion that seems to come out of nowhere. Sit quietly, and let your mind calm down. Then focus your attention on the emotion and ask yourself what it means and what it is trying to tell you. Take for example the anger that wells up when a man cuts in front of you in line. If you really look deeply, it will reveal a hidden meaning. It may, for example, be a deep-seated belief that the world is a threatening and dangerous place and you have to stand up for your rights and protect yourself at all costs. Or it may be telling you that all men are pushy and aggressive like your father, and they are not to be trusted. Whatever its message, it is vital that we take the time to pay attention and listen, or we will forever be thrown to and fro by the winds of our reactive emotions.

Buddhist psychology tells us that our sense of self is centered in the thinking mind and built up from language and thought, and Western social psychologists independently arrived at much the same conclusions. According to George Herbert Mead, the founder of the interactionist school of sociological analysis, "The self is not so much a substance as a process in which the conversation of gestures has been internalized within an organic form."[96] In other words, the self is nothing more than a pattern of thought—an internal conversation, reinforced in our interactions with other people, that constructs the world in terms of self and other.

If we look deeply, we will see that we carry on an almost nonstop self-dialogue. We congratulate ourselves when we do something we like and berate ourselves when we fail. Every event we experience is immediately evaluated for its potential impact on the self and what it tells us about who we are. When we feel slighted, we repeatedly review what the other person said and make up various stories about why they were wrong, while we savor each flattering remark that reinforces the way we want to see ourselves.

This "self-talk" of our thinking minds has a tremendous emotional charge. If the doctor tells us we have cancer, our thinking mind immediately spins out terrifying stories of our future suffering. If we win the lottery, images of the power and luxuries we will enjoy delight us. Even the minor everyday events that punctuate our lives are subject to constant self-evaluation and the positive or negative feelings they bring.

The teachings of the third turning tell us that we are all born with the predisposition toward this kind of "afflicted thinking" deep within our subconscious. Except when we are in the deepest states of meditation or are completely unconscious, this afflicted thinking is always going on, constantly manifesting the four afflictions: self-view, self-delusion, self-pride, and self-love.[97] This continuous feeling that "I am here, I am important" always lies beneath the activity of our discursive mind. Perhaps the greatest contribution of Western thought to the understanding of the psyche is the recognition that the self is also, at least in part, a social product. Mead, for example, holds that "The self is not something that exists first and then enters into relationship with others, but it is, so to speak, an eddy in the social current and so still a part of the current."[98]

Our sense of self is nurtured and encouraged right from our earliest years. It is said that at birth, infants draw no distinction between themselves and their environment. But they do have a tremendous capacity to learn, and children are taught to see the world in dualistic terms practically from the moment of their birth. As soon as we learn our first words, we are told that we are not Mommy, but Susie, Sally, or Sharon. We are taught that we are a girl not a boy, a child and not an adult, and on and on as the self thickens and strengthens. The languages we learn with their subjects and objects, "mes" and "yous," even the way they conjugate verbs, teach us the fundamental importance of self. And no matter what kind of language we use, the belief in self is built into the very foundations of the culture we assimilate. Each interaction we have with those around us reinforces the assumption of self until the belief in its solidity and importance becomes an unquestioned part of our habitual world.

The Dream, the Mystery, and the Silence

If we pay careful attention, it is quite possible to become aware of the various patterns and processes of our thinking mind, but the deeper layers of consciousness are a different matter. Very few of us have any direct knowledge of the subterranean flow of the subconscious mind that we have been discussing, nor are we aware of our original "pure" sensations for more than a fleeting instant before they are transformed by our habits and predispositions. We have had to rely on the great sutras, reflection, study, research, and the teachings of the most advanced yogis to put together our map of the psyche. And for most of us, it remains more of a useful theory than something we directly experience.

What we do experience directly is the endless flow of phenomena that arise in our awareness, which we have called the stream of consciousness. Images, ideas, sensations, and emotions succeed each other, one after the other, in a cascading stream that we appropriate as "my experience" in the ongoing story we tell about our lives. But what happens if we direct our attention away from the fascinating stories we weave about who we are and what we are doing, and focus directly on the phenomena we experience? What do we see? What is the true nature of phenomena?

In the *Sutra of the Explanation of the Profound Secrets*, the Buddha tells us that all the phenomena in this flowing stream of consciousness have three fundamental characteristics, which are called *parikalpita*, *paratantra,* and *parinishpanna* in Sanskrit. *Parikalpita* is usually translated as the "imagined" or "imputational" character. In a more poetic and evocative translation, Reb Anderson Roshi calls it "the dream." The point is that part of each thing we unenlightened beings perceive is imaginary—something that we project on to the world that isn't really there. As we saw in chapter 3, the sutra likens it to the cataracts in a blind man's eyes that distort everything he sees. But unlike cataracts, whose distortions are a more or less accidental result of physical damage to the eye, our mind actively works to construct and inhabit its delusions, and we will fight tenaciously to avoid giving them up. The result is that most of us live our entire lives in a dream: a dream of independence, autonomy, separation, and gain and loss—a dream of suffering.

Of course, everything we experience isn't pure delusion. When we gaze directly at reality and try to grasp it with our thoughts and concepts, we experience paratantra, the "other-dependent characteristic" of phenomena. The idea that phenomena are "other-dependent"—that each object depends on countless other causes and conditions outside itself for its existence—also implies another critical fact: impermanence. When the causes and conditions that create a phenomenon change, the phenomenon itself must change or disappear. Everything that arises must also cease.

Taken together, the teachings of impermanence and other-dependence are foundational principles for all the different schools of Buddhism. So it would be easy to assume that the other-dependence and impermanence of phenomena are their ultimate nature. But as profound as that idea is, it is still just an idea, an imputation. The teachings of the third turning tell us that the true nature of reality is completely inconceivable and ungraspable. The only way we can know the other-dependent is by confusing it with the ideas and concepts we project on to it. But in fact, it is completely inconceivable, a total enigma, what Anderson Roshi calls "the mystery."

Only when we stop confusing the ideas and concepts we project onto reality with reality itself, and we rest in the pure suchness of things just as they are, do we know parinishpanna—the "pattern of full perfection" or the "thoroughly established character" of phenomena. We might also call this the ultimate, the absolute, awakened buddha nature, or any one of a thousand other names, but whatever words we use, we run the danger of confusing them with reality itself. So for now, let's just call it "the silence"—not the silence that is the mere absence of sound, but the vast boundless silence that underlies all sound and appearance.[99]

Psychologically, what these great teachings tell us is that from the time we learn our first words until our final breath, our mind spins out an endless fantasy. We live in a dream dominated by the stories we tell about ourselves: stories about who we are, about what people think of us, about what we are going to do. We weave countless plots about how we will get what we want and avoid what we don't, and we worry about what will happen if they fail. Of course, we aren't the only ones in our dream. There are many others there too: friends, lovers, and enemies. There are people who help and support us, people who torment and afflict us, and countless others we see as the passive observers of our great drama. Animals, plants, supernatural beings, and just about anything else can also become part of the elaborate backdrop we paint for our personal drama. Yet no matter how enthralling, sooner or later our dreams will lead us into suffering; after all, they aren't actually real.

Some philosophers believe we are trapped in a solipsistic world of our own creation, but though each of us has our own individual dream, *we dream our dreams together*. The culture that succors us, defines our world, and shapes our aspirations is nothing more than a dream we share. It is, nonetheless, a uniquely powerful dream, and we ignore its awesome strength at our own peril. There is no surer way of being ostracized and excluded than threatening the dream your fellows share, whether by your speech, your actions, or even by mere accident. Ask the young man beaten to a pulp because he is "a queer," the rape victim turned out by her family because she was no longer "pure," or the refugee driven from her homeland because she refused to accept that her oppression was ordained by God. We are terrified that we might see our dreams for the illusions they are, and we protect them with bloody force.

But of course, it seldom has to go that far. The mere fact that everyone around us shares those dreams makes it likely that we will accept them without ever thinking much about it. If we do stray, we are told in countless subtle and not-so-subtle ways to get back on the path. A smirk, a cutting bit of sarcasm, or a cold stare quickly reminds us of the fate that waits those who threaten those cherished dreams. Such is the power of those dreams that few people see through them until they lead into a maelstrom of suffering, and even then, such insight is more the exception than the rule.

Beyond Psychology

The great psychological teachings of the sutras tell us that when a bodhisattva is wise with respect to the secrets of mind, thought, and consciousness, and sees the dream for what it is, she understands the origins of our suffering. She sees how our process of perception carves out images of separate individual objects from the seamless flow of existence, and the way we accept them as part of our taken-for-granted reality. She sees how the thinking mind generates the illusion of self and other. She sees the way this whole network of illusion arises from the predispositions of the subconscious mind, and how these illusions are nurtured and defended by the society in which we live. But a bodhisattva also realizes that even these teachings are still part of our dream, just a useful story we tell each other to help us find our way to liberation. Final liberation comes only when we rest in the true nature of our mind, undisturbed by any of our stories.

The Practice

Putting the View to Work

Intellectual understanding is only a first step toward realization. It shows us where to look, but it is only in practice that true discoveries are usually made. But if we can develop our intellectual understanding and our trust in the teachings, we can begin putting them to work long before we have the direct experience of the truth to which they point.

Some people develop deep faith in the teachings from the very first time they hear them. But most of us feel some doubt as well, and that can actually be a very healthy thing—it can push us to think more deeply. Buddhism comes to the West with a very different set of cultural assumptions than most secular Westerners, and it is only natural that we have some doubt and resistance. The key to sorting through this confusion and developing our confidence in the teachings is to really devote ourselves to studying them. We need to examine our doubts with our critical intelligence, keep an open mind, talk to our friends and teachers, read and reread the sutras, and perhaps most importantly look directly into our own experience. However we get there, as we grow more confident in the truth of the Buddha's words, they will become our guide and our refuge. When suffering arises, as it inevitably will, we will have their wisdom to support us.

Until we have had a direct experience of the truth of the Buddha's words, the Dharma is nonetheless likely to remain just one more story we tell ourselves. But it is a uniquely wholesome and profound story. When powerful afflictive emotions seem to well up out of the blue, we can remember the teachings about the alaya vijnana and the way such feelings arise from the seeds planted by our past actions and experiences, and then resolve to nurture the seeds of peace and harmony and stop watering those seeds of delusion. When we find ourselves trapped in the web of suffering spun by our narrow self-centered thoughts, the Dharma will be there to point us toward the truth: the separate little "me" we are trying so hard to protect is nothing but an illusion, and our deepest true nature is peace beyond all comprehension.

As we gain more clarity and understanding, we need to bring the Buddha's wisdom into our crisis-torn world as well as our individual lives. It seems that day by day, our planet becomes more fractious and divided. Countless groups concerned only with their own self-interest proclaim that they alone have the truth, and it is easy to respond with self-righteousness of our own. But the wisdom of the sutras reminds us that no ideologies, words, or beliefs, even those of the Buddha, can ever capture the ungraspable mystery of reality. We must let go of our fixed ideas and meet people on their own ground, with a commitment to work through our problems with love and compassion. And who knows, perhaps if we do that, we may even be an inspiration for others to do the same.

Acting with Virtue and Compassion

People in the West sometimes think that meditation is all that Buddhism is really about. But the sutras tell us again and again that the way we live our lives is incredibly important. Each positive action we do plants the seeds of peace and liberation, and each negative action plants the seeds of suffering. As the Buddha said in the first turning of the wheel:

I am the owner of my actions, heir to my actions, born of my actions, related through my actions, and have my actions as my arbitrator. Whatever I do, for good or for evil, to that will I fall heir.[100]

It is a very simple truth: act with virtue and compassion, and your life will become more peaceful and joyous; act with hatred and selfishness, and you will grow a garden of suffering. Yet putting that wisdom into practice in our daily lives is anything but simple. The habit energies we have built up propel us into harmful and deluded actions without us ever realizing what we are doing, and even when we try to bring mindful attention to our actions, we may still not know the best way to respond to the endless challenges of life. As our meditation practice gradually helps us to calm and clarify the muddy waters of our deluded mind, acting with virtue and compassion becomes easier and easier until ultimately it is virtually automatic. But in the meantime, the sutras offer us some wise guidelines to help point the way for us.

Some of the most important signposts are, as we saw in chapter 1, the five precepts that lay Buddhists are traditionally expected to follow: to abstain from harming living beings, stealing, sexual misconduct, harmful speech, and intoxication. But it is important to remember that these are not absolute rules or the commands of an all-powerful God, as we often believe in the West, but guidelines for reflection and study. They point out key areas of our lives that we need to pay close attention to, and they provide help when we are unsure of the right thing to do. But blindly following the precepts is no substitute for mindful awareness and reflection. It may sometimes be necessary to lie, steal, or even kill, but if we do violate the precepts, we must do it only with the most careful attention to the situation, the welfare of all concerned, and our own motivation.

Of course, virtuous behavior involves a lot more than just avoiding doing harm to ourselves or others. We need to work for the benefit of "all sentient beings"—ourselves, our friends and relations, and all the other people and animals with whom we share our world. We need, in other words, to act with the boundless love and compassion of the bodhisattvas. That can seem like a pretty daunting task for most of us, but even small acts of kindness and compassion are important. Every action full of loving kindness strengthens our seeds of compassion, and makes us more likely to act with the virtue of a boundless heart in the future.

Meditation

No other aspect of the Buddha's teachings has so captured the Western imagination as meditation practice. Whether their inspiration is the explosive power of the kung fu master, the inner beauty of the accomplished yogini, or the loving compassion of someone like the Dalai Lama, Westerners are starting to feel that meditation has something important to offer them. Fifty years ago, on the other hand, meditation was seen as an eccentric practice limited to the bohemian fringes of society. Now it is looked upon as something practical, even sophisticated. And such views are backed up by a growing body of scientific research showing that meditation is an effective way to calm down and to cope with the ever-mounting stress of postmodern life.

It is hard to overemphasize the importance of these changes in attitudes for our society and our lives. Yet there is still a danger that the deepest spiritual goals of meditation practice will get lost amid all this new attention. One of the best ways to insure that doesn't happen is to root our practice in the timeless wisdom of the classic sutras. The sutras present meditation practice as an essential part of the journey of awakening—something that is deep, powerful, and profound—but at the same time, they show that meditation is not an end in itself, that it does not stand apart from the rest of the path. Virtuous and compassionate behavior, right understanding and wisdom, and meditation practice make up a seamless whole, each one interpenetrating and supporting the others. Without right understanding, our meditation practice is likely to flounder, and the tranquility and wisdom that meditation can bring will escape us if we live loveless lives full of selfishness or hatred.

The great sutras of the three turnings give us instructions for a host of meditation practices, and over the centuries different Buddhist traditions have added a wide array of other meditation techniques. In the Vajrayana tradition another vast body of texts known as the tantras pass on complex visualization and ritual practices. To make matters more complicated, many contemporary teachers have freely modified traditional practices to make them more suitable for their Western students or have created entirely new meditations of their own. Many teachers of mindfulness meditation have gone so far as to entirely separate themselves from the Buddhist tradition in order to appeal to a more secular audience.

This situation can be pretty bewildering for many students. A strong meditation practice is a vital part of the spiritual path, but there are so many different practices it is hard to know which to choose or how to do them correctly. The easiest way to navigate these waters is to find a trusted teacher to help guide us along the way. But the combination of our deeply ingrained individualism with the mass literacy and instant communications of the industrial era has meant that many Westerners are practicing the Dharma completely on their own without the support of teachers or a sangha of fellow practitioners. Although many traditionalists would describe that as a futile or even dangerous endeavor, some of these solitary seekers have unquestionably gained great realization. Even though it must have been far less common, this approach was not unknown even in traditional cultures of ancient Asia. The sutras call those who have attained a deep realization on this path *pratyekabuddhas*. But while the sutras give these "solitary buddhas" great respect and admiration, their path is still considered a lesser vehicle, for they lack the boundless compassion of the great bodhisattva who dedicates herself to the benefit of all sentient begins. Of course, few of us need to worry about attaining either level of realization in this lifetime, but as a practical matter, there is little doubt that working with a genuine teacher and a supportive sangha usually makes the journey faster, easier, and safer.

Just because a teacher is well known and respected does not, however, necessarily mean they are the right teacher for you. Teachers generally teach what they have learned from their particular tradition and personal history, and the guidance you are given often depends as much on the background of the teacher as your own unique needs. So it is important to look carefully before committing yourself to a teacher and the path they follow to make sure you have a deep and genuine connection, and to remember that Buddhist teachers, like anyone else, can still abuse their power and position.

The next two chapters show us how two great Western teachers, Reb Anderson Roshi and Lama Palden Drolma, bring the teachings of the sutras to life for their students and transform them into practical guidance for their meditation practice. Although Anderson Roshi comes from the Zen tradition and Lama Palden from the Vajrayana, the course of their lives shows remarkable similarities. They both have shown a life-long interest in spirituality, their lives were both profoundly transformed in their middle twenties when they met their root teacher and committed themselves to a lifetime of Buddhist practice and teaching, and they both went on to have a profound impact not only on the lives of their many students but on the course of Western Buddhism. Both chapters are based on their spontaneous Dharma talks, which I have edited down into a more publishable form. They not only show how to put the wisdom of the sutras into practical use, but they also give us a feeling for some of the differences between these traditions and of the great benefits we can gain from working closely with a good teacher.

5

Tasting the Truth
of the Buddha's Words:
A Zen Perspective

By Reb Anderson Roshi

One of the most famous chants in the Zen tradition ends with a vow to "taste the truth of the Buddha's words." Reading the great sutras or hearing our teachers explain them to us is a rare and amazing event. Having them to listen to, accept, and remember is wonderful. But sometimes when we hear the truth, we don't necessarily *taste* it. And according to this chant, it is actually possible to taste it in our body. Even as we walk around and live our daily lives, we can remember what we heard, and we can taste the truth of those words in the deepest parts of our being. When we do that, the Buddha's teachings take over our body and mind, and we become the teaching.

The Path of Practice: Wisdom and Compassion

The way we come to taste the truth of the Buddha's words is sometimes called the path of practice or the process of meditation. First, we read the sutras or hear the teachings, and then by doing various meditation practices, we let the teachings into our body and mind more and more deeply. In Sanskrit and Pali that process is sometimes called *bhavana.* Bhavana is a general term that can be translated as "cultivation" or "meditation." But etymologically, bhavana derives from the word *bhava,* which means "to be," so the point of Buddhist meditation really is to become a buddha. When we taste the truth of the Tathagata's words, we feel we have become the Buddha.

There is another chant that ends "The Buddha Way is unsurpassable. I vow to become it." The Buddha way is the way of peace, the way of reconciliation, the way of compassion. Buddhism holds up the possibility that if we can become wise like the Buddha, then we can help other people free themselves of their fear and hatred by teaching them how to awaken to Buddha's wisdom. Because of Buddha's wisdom, he loved all beings. He was not afraid of anyone, nor did he hate anyone. Of course, some people weren't ready to hear his teachings, but he helped countless others. And he continued to love those he couldn't help, because it is the job of the wise person to be patient with those who learn slowly. The Buddha's wisdom is the final solution to hatred and fear, but it is practiced together with Buddha's compassion.

The teachings of the second and third turnings distill the instructions for all the practices of wisdom and compassion down to six essential points: the six perfections. The entire Buddhist path and all the teachings can be summarized in these six categories. The first five perfections—generosity, ethical behavior, patience, diligence, and meditative concentration—are all compassion practices. They help us make all our relationships, whether with people, animals, or even inanimate objects, into expressions of loving-kindness and concern. When we practice these perfections, we generate the desire to care for all things and to free all beings from their ignorance and the suffering it causes.

These compassion practices teach us how to relate to our own body and mind and the bodies and minds of others. However, the sixth perfection, wisdom, is different. Rather than teaching us how to relate to things, the wisdom teachings focus on the nature of the things themselves—the nature of phenomena. Once we have the correct understanding of phenomena, we bring that wisdom into our other practices to purify our compassion.

Of course, we should try to practice generosity, ethical discipline, patience, diligence, and concentration even before we have wisdom. But if we don't understand the nature of phenomena, it's difficult to do the compassion practices correctly, because we start clinging to their results. So it is a two-way street. Buddha's wisdom grows out of our compassion, and at the same time it purifies and strengthens our compassion. It transforms our compassion into the Buddha's compassion, which unleashes our full potential to bring peace and harmony to the world.

Practicing Concentration

Both wisdom and compassion are really types of meditation, but a lot of people only think about the fifth perfection, concentration, when they think about meditation. Perhaps that is because our lives are often hectic and confused, and concentration meditation helps us become more tranquil and more present with what is happening. Whatever the reason this type of meditation is so popular, it is vitally important because it makes us flexible, relaxed, and buoyant, so that we can do all the other compassion and wisdom practices.

When we are calm and concentrated, we are on "temporary leave" from affliction, because we give up involvement in the discursive thinking that creates our suffering. Etymologically, *discursive* means "running about" or "coursing about." So discursive thought is the type of thought in which we're running about, wandering around in our head. When we practice giving it up, we practice the stabilization of the mind. When some object appears in awareness, we train ourselves not to grasp it or its characteristics or get too involved with it. We're just aware, and that's all. Being with objects without grasping their characteristics is the way we realize tranquility. So it isn't that we intentionally calm the mind, but that we find the way for the mind to be calm with what it knows. As we move away from the grasping that creates disturbance and agitation, we move into a different way of being. This is why this kind of practice is also called tranquility meditation.

Another way to put it is that we just accept what's given and that's it. Whatever objects are presented to awareness, whether they are concepts, sense perceptions, or anything else, we just accept them as they're given. No embellishment. Training the attention to be with the process of knowing in this very basic and intimate way calms us and prevents unwholesome states from arising. Until we've realized insight and understand the true nature of phenomena, the potential for such states to arise is still there. As soon as we start grasping or embellishing things again, we open the doors to the unwholesome states and the agitation they cause.

When we enter into a state that's calm, alert, and concentrated, we're saying basically, "I accept whatever is given." There's a gratitude in that kind of mind, and there's a kind of generosity too, because we give up all the tendencies to elaborate and argue. We make a gift of our distractions. We give our imagination away. We don't kill it. We just give it away.

When something comes up when we're doing this kind of meditation, the practice is just to give up discursive thought about it. If we become aware of our posture, for example, we give up the thought that our posture is good or bad. We give up thinking that our posture isn't as good as the person sitting next to us or that it is better. We just experience our posture in whatever way we experience it—that's it. When we hear the sound of a bird, we don't think it's a good-sounding bird or a bad-sounding bird. When we have a painful sensation, we don't think that it's more painful than before or less painful than before, or wonder about how long it will be painful, what we did to make it happen, or why it is happening to us. We give up wandering around among all our thoughts and all the different objects of our experience. The *Sutra of the Explanation of the Profound Secrets* refers to this kind of tranquility meditation as paying attention to the "uninterrupted mind" or the "mind contemplated by any mind." For it is not as if there is nothing there when we give up discursive thought; what remains is the mind uninterrupted by thought.

Developing Insight

Even when we give up discursive thought and are tranquil and calm, we don't necessarily become wise. In fact, there are ways of *using* discursive thought that can help us gain true insight; in the end, the path is to join the fruit of giving up discursive thought with the fruit of using discursive thought. In other words, we join wisdom and tranquility together. And in that unity of wisdom and tranquility, a supreme wisdom arises—the wisdom in which we actually *become* the teaching.

I always try to encourage people to be inspired and enthusiastic about learning to use our wandering mind to develop wisdom, because I think we need some encouragement. My general impression from looking into my own mind, and hearing about other people's experiences, is that there is often a lot of difficulty in practicing wisdom. Practicing tranquility is sometimes difficult at the start too, but after we give up discursive thought, it's not so difficult anymore. Practicing wisdom, however, often continues to be difficult almost to the very highest levels. But no matter how difficult, wisdom meditation is essential, because concentration meditation alone does not overthrow our deep misconceptions about the world. And until we completely overthrow those deep misconceptions, we are always vulnerable to misunderstanding and confusion, because we don't see what is happening clearly. Only when we finally realize Buddha's wisdom are we able to look at reality without veering off to the right or to the left, and see things exactly as they are.

But facing reality is hard, because we are so used to ignoring it. In fact, we are actually born to look away from it. It requires a major reorientation to somehow coax ourselves into hearing the teachings about the way things are and applying them to our actual experience right now. So first we need to hear, study, and contemplate the Buddha's teachings about impermanence and the true characteristics of phenomena. Once we have heard them over and over again, studied them deeply, and contemplated them in our meditation, then we apply those teaching to what is happening right now, both in our meditation and in our daily life.

Fortunately, wisdom meditation can be done more easily in everyday life than tranquility meditation. That is because we can do insight work while we are talking. In fact, we usually need to talk to ourselves while we are doing insight work, because we need to be constantly repeating the teachings of the buddhas and bodhisattvas that we have heard and read, and checking to see if things are really the way the teachings say they are. Even if we can't see the truth of the teachings right away, if we just think about things being that way, we can still make progress.

By studying and meditating on the teachings the Buddha left us in the great sutras, we learn to use discursive thought to help us to see through our illusions and experience things the way they really are. But that is quite a different type of meditation than giving up discursive thought. Wisdom is the fruit of using discursive thought and tranquility is the fruit of giving it up, and we need to do both types of meditation.

Practicing Tranquility and Insight Together

It may seem surprising, but in the early phases of insight work we don't want to be too calm. We need some concentration, but we can't continue the investigation when we're too calm because we don't have any thoughts. When the insight is established, however, and we're not really doing the analysis anymore, then we bring that understanding into a state of intense concentration and calm, and it penetrates the deepest parts of our mind and body.

Part of the reason we need help from a teacher is to know when to switch from one type of meditation to another. Even if we're calm and peaceful when we start doing insight work, we are likely to become more agitated and excited, especially at the first levels of insight. A lot of people become agitated in a negative way when they think they don't understand. On the other hand, some people are excited in a positive way. They feel good because they think they do understand, so they're energized and their mind is zipping around. If we get really excited about how wonderful it is that we understand these teachings or if we're really depressed and discouraged that we don't understand them, then it's probably a good idea to put aside our insight work for a while and calm down. But we can be confident that doing so is part of the course of developing wisdom; we're not wasting our time if we need to calm down a little bit. So if we feel too upset, we just go back to the calming work again. And if we're upset about our calming meditation not working, then we just give up our thoughts that it's not working. Our evaluations of our meditation are just more discursive thoughts to give up and let go of.

What's the difference in the way we practice tranquility meditation and the way we practice insight meditation? Let's say I'm meditating and I notice my hand. The stabilization practice that produces tranquility requires us to focus on being with the hand in a certain way. The practice is to know it without grasping its characteristics; to know it without elaborating on it by saying it's a clean hand, it's a man's hand, or whatever. Of course, in the next moment I might think, "It is a man's hand." But what I am looking at then is a *concept* of a man's hand. And if that's given to me, I accept it too, and don't grasp it, don't elaborate on it, and don't say "I'm not supposed to think I am looking at a man's hand." I just realize that is just another concept, another object I'm aware of, and I try not to slip on it anymore. Nongrasping and nonelaboration are the way of being in tranquility meditation.

Now suppose that I'm successful in my calming meditation. I'm being very steady, and things have gotten very simple for me. I actually see that I'm not slipping. I just see thing after thing after thing, object after object. I let each one be without grasping it. And then either I intentionally shift, perhaps at the suggestion of my teacher, or something happens and my attention spontaneously changes. I shift from trying to be with everything in the same way to contemplating the objects of my attention in order to see what they really are. I look to see what the object is, how the object exists. Since I need to continue in this nongrasping way, I don't want to get attached to the object's characteristics in this meditation either, but I will start to notice its characteristics and to contemplate them.

When we have trained for a while and entered into a state of calm that contemplates what's out there, we start to see things directly that we only knew intellectually before. We've all heard, for example, that we're going to die. We know that cups break, that cars break. We know that other people get sick and die. We know that things change and that all compounded phenomena are impermanent. But the way that touches us when we're calm is much deeper than the way it touches us when our mind is jumping around in an agitated state.

When we first hear about the impermanence of phenomena and how it causes suffering, we may not understand. But as we hear more about it, and think about it over and over again, it will finally sink in: whatever changes is painful. And when we get it, we change. Our mind and body are transformed. Then, if we keep up with this work, keep thinking about it, and keep applying it to various new situations, we're transformed again and again at ever-deeper levels.

Yet until the work of transformation is complete, we're still afflicted by the impermanence of things, and that is why tranquility meditation is such an important part of this process. When we enter into the one-pointedness of the calm mind, the affliction is temporarily alleviated. We get to look at things and see what is usually painful without the pain. Then we're not so afraid to really open up to the reality of impermanence, because it's not going to hurt us to see it.

Even if we don't admit it, we probably still expect that at least some things really will be solid and dependable. Since we know that doesn't accord with the Buddha's teachings, we may pretend that we don't think that way. But sooner or later something will break or someone will die, and we realize that at some level we really did expect that they would always be around. So even though we still, deep down, hold the view that things are permanent, we're also had an insight and we realize that view is just another groundless belief. So during our meditation, we look at that view, we at our realization, and then juxtapose them. We see that phenomena are impermanent, but we still have the view that things are permanent. So now we get very calm and look again, and we confirm that everything really is impermanent and that our belief in permanence really is nonsense. Ordinarily we probably would be afraid to see the real truth, but because we are temporarily in a calm, fearless state, we're not afraid to see things the way they really are. Practicing in this way, these deep misconceptions can be uprooted and cleared away. And then, even if we're not in a state of calm, the afflictions don't come up, because we have uprooted the beliefs that cause them.

Day by day, as we alternate between tranquility and insight practice, we settle more and more deeply into our meditation, and the teachings penetrate to ever-deeper levels. Then, if we're following the path laid out in the third turning, at some point we make another pivot. Either because our teacher says we're ready, or because a conviction spontaneously arises that the time is right, we turn and contemplate another doctrine: the calm, undisturbed mind that is the object of our concentration meditation and the objects of our discursive mind that we use in our insight work—in other words, what appears as the inner and outer world—are really just one mind. All our ideas and thoughts about the doctrine, our practice, impermanence, or anything else, and any objects that appear—including the breath we concentrate on and the calm, uninterrupted mind that holds them—are all only consciousness.

Suppose, for example, we are looking at something, say a person's face, a painful sensation, or a tree. If we give up discursive thought and don't pay attention to the particular characteristics of the phenomena that are arising, we become calm, pliant, and concentrated. Then if we use our calm, concentrated mind to apply those teachings to the objects we are contemplating, it may dawn on us that what we're actually looking at is just mind appearing as a face, or mind appearing as a painful sensation, or mind appearing as a tree. No matter what objects the mind contemplates, no matter what it is paying attention to, mind is actually paying attention to mind itself. Practicing in this way, we are not just doing tranquility meditation or insight meditation, we are practicing the two combined.

When we finally come to a deep existential understanding of the great truth of these teachings, concentration and insight—or, if you will, compassion and wisdom—are not just combined, they are unified into what the *Sutra of the Explanation of the Profound Secrets* calls the one-pointed mind: "the realization that: 'This image which is the focus of concentration is cognition-only.' Having realized that, it is mental attention to suchness."[101] With this culminating realization, all effort drops away and we rest in pure suchness: the blissful perfection of the way things truly are.

Working with the Hindrances

The path to realization is usually a long one, and many hindrances are likely to arise to block our way. If we're able to train our attention, calm our mind, and work with what happens without grasping it, then those hindrances are temporarily suspended. As long as we're clear and focused, they don't come up. But if we slip even just for a moment and let our thoughts start elaborating, a crack opens and the hindrances flood in. For example, when we settle into a tranquil stare, the thought may occur that "This is really a wonderful feeling." And that kind of embellishment opens the door to clinging and lusting for more of those states. So what should we do when these hindrance arise?

The basic idea is to just let things be, so if we're grasping, we let ourself grasp. We accept what's given, and sometimes what's given is the awareness that we're grasping. We don't punish ourselves for that. We just say, "This is happening." We don't say, "Whoopee!" or "Oh no!"— just, "Here's grasping." That's enough. If we do more than that, we open the door for the five hindrances to block our way.

The first hindrance is desire. It could be the desire for that calm meditative state, for some kind of nice experience, for sex, for love, or for an endless array of other objects our mind creates. The second hindrance is ill will. We might, for example, start thinking that some state we are in isn't so good and start feeling ill will toward somebody we think is to blame for it. The next hindrance is the sloth and torpor that seem to rob us of the energy to pursue our practice. The fourth hindrance is restlessness and worry, and the last one is doubt, particularly doubt about the truth of the Dharma or about our ability to realize it.

My favorite way of dealing with the hindrances is just to let them in to my practice and keep on meditating. If we notice these hindrances coming up, we don't grasp them or get involved exploring their cause or characteristics. Just accept them as they're given—that's it. Then we're back on track again; the hindrances are disarmed, and we're just going back to our meditation practice, rather than doing some big recovery program. But that is not easy to do, because the hindrances are more difficult to accept than most other things. It isn't hard to let colors, music, or most physical sensations and thoughts just be what they are. But when the hindrances arise, we feel like they're bad and we have to do something about them. They are sticky and difficult to let go of, and when we try to push them away, they just come back.

So if we feel we just can't get back to our regular practice, there are also specific practices that are recommended as antidotes for each different hindrance. For example, suppose we're troubled by sensual desire and it's really disrupting our meditation, so we want to do something to directly address the problem. Generally, most kinds of sensual desires aren't really high-quality aesthetic involvements, but more just wallowing in pleasure. There're just laziness, or greediness, and not really in accord with what we sat down to do. So we just need to get serious. When I used to have these kinds of experiences, I would think of my teacher when he died. I'd just remember what he looked like lying on the ground dead, and that would usually snap me out of it. And if that didn't work, I would get a little gorier. In the traditional books, they have some very gruesome subjects to think about. For example, if just thinking of some serious moment in our life, like when our mother or father died, doesn't refocus our mind, then we might envision the person we think is so attractive as a rotting corpse full of maggots and worms. But it is best not to go into that kind of thing unless nothing else seems to work.

The main thing we do for the hindrance of ill will is to practice loving-kindness—which is also a concentration practice. As we work at it, we direct the loving-kindness toward ourselves and toward any other object of ill will we may have. We just keep making an effort over and over again, sending out loving-kindness until we get ourselves free of all those feelings.

There are a lot of ways to respond to sloth and torpor, but the basic approach is to remember our aspiration. Remember why we are doing the practice and reaffirm our commitment to helping all those suffering beings, who are in such great need. Once we have renewed our aspiration, we should try to bring some lightness and enthusiasm back to our practice. But although aspiration is the real remedy for this hindrance, sometimes resting is another important part of the solution, because rest is key to enthusiasm. So it's also okay to take a nap, go for a walk, or splash cold water on our face.

The antidote for restlessness and worry is to follow our breath even if we weren't doing breath meditation. Whatever concepts we're worrying about, move away from them and put our attention on the breath.

Worry will go away as soon as our conceptual thinking does. Some people believe that they have a lot of things they have to worry about, but worry is an unwholesome dharma. It doesn't help us. To be concerned for people, to care about people, isn't the same as worrying. And the same thing is true for agitation. It doesn't get us anywhere, and if we focus on our breath, we calm down and the agitation dissolves.

Then there is doubt. When we're doing the practice wholeheartedly, we don't have any question about it. We appreciate what we're doing. But when we don't do it wholeheartedly, we get in trouble, and we may start wondering, "Is this practice really worth my effort? Is it really good to be doing this?" If any concerns like that come up, talk to a teacher. The teacher may say that doubts arise because we are not doing the practice wholeheartedly, and tell us to go back and keep at it. But they may give us new instructions or suggest another approach. There are also books we can read that describe the benefits of practice, or we can talk to others in our community and hear firsthand accounts of the enormous rewards that come from following the Buddhist path. After that, we can reason with ourselves until we have a sense of confidence and certainty in the benefits of the practice, and then go back to work.

Physical illness isn't one of the five hindrances, but any one of the traditional five could develop if we don't accept illness with the spirit of no-embellishment. The sickness itself isn't the problem—our response to it is. If we're coughing and having trouble breathing, we may veer off into ill will. We may start getting worried or angry about our sickness, or doubt the value of practicing while we're sick, and things like that. There are practices for people who are sick, but it is the aversion to sickness that those practices try to cure, not the illness itself.

If we just accept our sickness the way it is, we can be very calm and very loving to ourselves when we're sick. And then in sickness we can sometimes have a great insight. It's true that it may be hard to practice when we're ill, because we don't have enough energy to stay awake and pay attention to the phenomena that arise and to notice whether we're working with them correctly. But when we don't have enough energy to pay attention, that's the hindrance. It's the lack of energy, not the illness.

It's possible we might slip into sloth when we're sick, but some people are quite energetic and alert in their sickness and not slothful at all. If we do feel tired, it is usually a good thing to rest, because that is often the best way to take care of our body. Of course, there are stories of monks who kept pushing themselves even when they were sick and had a great realization. But it can also work out very badly, because many unwholesome states can arise if we don't rest when we need to.

There are also a couple of general antidotes that can be used with any of the hindrances. One is to develop a sense of self-respect and decorum. Let's say we've made arrangements to go to a retreat, but one way or another we're goofing off. We're not doing our work, and we're afflicted by hindrances like sloth, ill will, and doubt. We are, in a sense, out of self-respect and decorum. Our friends and family have supported us to do this, people are feeding us to do this, and we've made special arrangements to do this, so a sense of decorum would tell us that it's appropriate that we would do it now. People will be disappointed in us if we set up this special situation and don't do the work. Moreover, if we develop a sense of self-respect, we will know we can do better than we're doing. We'll know we can go back to the meditation and that we don't have to be wallowing in these unwholesome states.

This kind of self-respect can be stimulated by shame or guilt. "This is beneath me." "I can do better than this." "I don't have to do sloppy work here." Those kinds of thoughts push us to do better. We may also be afraid that people will be disappointed in us and that we are letting them down. They set up this meditation class for us, and our family's doing childcare so we can be here, but we're not using the opportunity.

There are Zen stories in which the teacher sees that the monks have fallen completely asleep. The teacher says, "You know, people are out there in the hot sun, growing rice to feed you, and they're giving you this rice so that you will understand yourself and become a beneficial person in this world, and here you are eating their rice and sleeping. You should be ashamed of yourselves." And sometimes the teachers get a lot harsher than that. But whatever their response, there's something to it. We shouldn't need to be reminded that we're being supported to meditate. Being able to meditate is a great opportunity. Say thank you and use it. Don't waste a lot of time. We should expect that of ourselves, and we should know that other people expect that of us too.

The other general antidote is to directly suppress the hindrance. If we say, "Just stop this anger trip, just stop hating, just stop worrying, just stop doubting, just stop it," and make sure to say it with kindness, the hindrance doesn't turn into ill will toward ourself or the experiences we are encountering. We want to say it in a clear, helpful way to remind ourself of what we're doing and to respect the efforts we have already made.

We've got to be careful with these antidotes. They should all be done with this spirit of loving-kindness, so that we can do them over and over again without feeling we're harming ourselves by this training. The goal is to help us calm down and feel relaxed and at peace. Don't get heavy or oppressive, so we can return to our original practice with grace and ease.

To really taste the truth of the Buddha's words, we have to do more than just read the sutras. We have to memorize them, recite them, and study them. We need to practice the perfections of generosity, ethical behavior, patience, and diligence. We have to train ourselves in concentration so that we become calm, buoyant, and joyful, use skillful means to handle our hindrances, and finally we have to use that calm, concentrated mind to see directly into the true nature of all things and develop wisdom. It can be a long journey, but it is the most important one we will ever take.

6

Envisioning Tara:
A Vajrayana Perspective

By Lama Palden Drolma

Zen and Vajrayana may appear to be strikingly different, but they are both built on the same teachings, on the same three turnings of the wheel. Zen teachers often express things in one way and Vajrayana teachers in another, but they draw upon the same essential understanding. Of course, a lot of people don't realize this, because they haven't studied the teachings. But it's extremely important for us to have some philosophical understanding, some precision. Then wherever we stand, whatever we believe or don't believe, at least we have some clarity.

If we study Buddhist philosophy and practice it to the point where we really gain direct, experiential understanding, there is a profound shift in the way we structure reality. We come to understand how to orient our practice and how to integrate it with our daily life. When problems come up, we know how to deal with them.

But it's important that we both study philosophy and engage with our spiritual practice; not just one or the other. No matter how much practice we do, it isn't likely to have much impact on our view of reality unless we also have some philosophical understanding. But without practice, we won't really understand the philosophy. We have to really study, and we have to really practice, or it doesn't all make sense. In fact, the way it is taught in Vajrayana, the three turnings of the wheel are the stages in the development of our practice as we progress along the path.

At the same time, however, Buddhism isn't just dogma that we are supposed to believe in. Of course, its philosophy is sophisticated and highly developed, but we are not encouraged to just hear something and believe it just because we are told it is true. Once we hear the teachings, we need to contemplate them and then investigate our own experience and find out what is true inside ourselves.

This is what faith is in Buddhism. Faith is not just some kind of blind acceptance of the teachings based on hope, fear, or tradition. We do not leave our rational mind at the door. True faith has other sources. It begins with a kind of openheartedness that allows us to be receptive to new ideas and experiences. It may, for example, arise when we hear someone like the Dalai Lama speak, or when we meet some other spiritual person and are inspired by them. Or perhaps our inspiration may come from nature when we suddenly come into a deep sense of oneness with all that is. When something like that touches our heart, it is called the faith of inspiration. Something feels really right about it, and it may get us going in a new direction. Then later, if we start working with a teacher and progressing along the path, a new kind of faith may arise when the teachings begin resonating with something deep inside us and we start to feel their effects on us. Finally, we develop the unshakable faith of knowingness when we actually have a direct experience of the truth the teachings describe.

Take, for example, the teachings on rebirth. The idea that we don't just have one life, that we've had countless lives before and will probably have more in the future, is one of the most fundamental teachings in the sutras and throughout all Asian Buddhism. Even though I never mentioned it to anyone, as a small child, I remembered past lives, so it wasn't ever a question for me. I didn't know we weren't supposed to believe in them. But whether or not we believe in this teaching isn't the essential point; none of the teachings is something we have to accept on blind faith. Such beliefs do not help. They just add to our pile of concepts. It's a question of what we come to know is true, and that will happen in its own time, whenever our understanding ripens.

The Spiritual Path

Meditation is becoming more and more popular here in the West. People like it because it can give us a breather from our super busy, chaotic lives. They are also finding out that it can help them deal with all the pain and difficulties they inevitably encounter in their lives. But that's not really the goal of Buddhist practice, or for that matter, of any true spiritual path. It's not intended to just make us feel a little better, be less stressed, be more at ease. Although these are all benefits of meditation, they are not the goal itself. Of course, we want to work on our character and develop more patience, loving-kindness, and generosity. But the purpose of this work is far, far beyond that.

The ultimate goal is not to make ourselves into better people. It's to uncover who and what we actually are. It's to bring ourselves to complete and total liberation, which means that we are no longer at the mercy of any phenomena. We no longer experience a contradiction between life and death; between having a body and not having a body; between being in a very, very difficult situation or being in a very peaceful, wonderful situation. The path is to uncover our innermost purity, not to make ourselves into something we aren't. That way it's not just a temporary fix. We're looking for a permanent and complete solution, not a temporary solution just to help us endure this life as best we can. Then our mind can be at peace and full of compassion and wisdom regardless of the circumstances.

As we saw in the *Tathagatagarbha Sutra*, our authentic true nature is often likened to gold. But it's the kind of gold you might find deep in a mountain with many other ores wrapped around it, so it's not always easy to see. Our work on the spiritual path helps us refine the ore of our lives and clear away the other elements, so that our true nature shines forth in its golden beauty. Then we can experience our pure being that was always there from the beginning but was hidden from view. Until we do that, we can't fully experience the freedom, joy, and peace that abide at the core of our being. We call this experience "awakening to our true nature," and it empowers us to be of benefit to all beings everywhere. This timeless awareness is always innately there. Just like the gold covered by ore, our true nature is masked by our delusions. But also like the gold, it is always pure and unsullied.

My job as a teacher is to help people open to their true nature and to clear away the stuff that's in the way. One of the wonderful things about this work is seeing people awaken and flower into who they truly are. Everybody is completely unique in the way they manifest their awakening. One person might dedicate themselves to teaching others, another might go to live in the solitude of the mountains, while someone else might not appear to change much at all from the outside, but their inner reality has been liberated.

Whatever hardships we go through, whatever struggles we face with the shadowy parts of ourselves, it is all worth it in the end. The hard work necessary to release our habitual patterns of delusion brings us ever-increasing peace and well-being. As we go further and further along the way, we're able to be of true benefit to others and to ourselves. Then whatever else we want to do with this life is empowered through our blossoming. As the ore falls away, the gold of our true buddha nature is just radiantly there.

On the way, we have to learn to trust our own discerning wisdom. Suppose, for example, we're picking up something enticing from a spiritual teacher or we're thinking about embarking on some new path, and we're not quite sure what to do. A part of us is saying yes and another part is kind of hesitant. We need to learn to distinguish an emotional reaction from a real intuition. It's possible that we're hesitating because we are picking up something that could be a real problem, or maybe it's just that our ego is resistant to change. We need to learn to trust our own innate wisdom for it is the key to successfully navigating all the difficulties of the spiritual path and of our lives as human beings.

This discernment is part of what Buddhists call "skillful means"— being able to deal with our lives skillfully in order to be of benefit to others. For example, as we practice, the mind comes to calm abiding more and more often. In that state we can bring in patience when we're frustrated and kindness when we're irritated or angry. When we're stingy, we bring in more generosity. When we work with ourselves with such skillful means, we come closer to truth; we come closer to the primordial goodness of who we truly are. Instead of merely responding to life out of our old habitual patterns, we respond with conscious awareness of the situation we are in and the ways in which we are interacting with others. Then we have a real choice in how we behave. For those who have reached full realization, skillful action arises spontaneously on the spot, but for most of us the essence of skillful means involves stepping back before we act and contemplating what is the best action for everyone in each difficult situation. Skillful means require that we don't act from mere self-concern but because we want what is the best for all beings involved.

Of course, it isn't always obvious what kind of behavior is skillful. Sometimes a mentor might come down on us in a really wrathful way that pushes all our buttons. But instead of just reacting from our old habits, we need to look carefully and be open to the possibility that her actions are actually skillful means to help us wake up. The same thing can happen if you are practicing with friends or in a spiritual community. If we fall on our faces in the mud, the others need to respond with compassion and wisdom. But the most skillful means may be to just bluntly tell us something we don't really want to hear. The most loving response isn't always warm and fuzzy.

Understanding Ego

The ego has gotten a bad rap in some spiritual circles. Since the teachings tell us that the ego is insubstantial, unreal, and illusory, some people think that if they kill their ego everything will be fine. But personally, I believe that's completely off the mark. First of all, I haven't seen anybody who has been able to kill their ego, and moreover, such attitudes foster a kind of violence and self-estrangement. Rather than viewing the ego as some kind of enemy, we should look at it more as a child in need of a lot of love and guidance.

The ego usually develops between the ages of three and six, so its operating system is based on old information, a lot of which is out of date. The ego is actually trying to help us, but it just doesn't have the right information or the right understanding. It's a natural part of the psyche of any human being, but it usually is fairly untrained, lacking in sufficient knowledge and insight, and a little bit uncivilized.

Years ago I heard A. H. Almaas, the author and mystic who started the Diamond Approach, say that we all go to enlightenment kicking and screaming, and I thought that was so right. Sometimes the ego is in such total rebellion against our spiritual practice that it's almost like a child throwing a fit. The ego just wants to do what it wants to do and that's it. And underneath, there's usually a lot of fear, because of the enormous implications of deep spiritual practice. The ego, especially in the deep unconscious, is afraid of the implications of the spiritual journey. It is afraid it will have to take on a lot more responsibility, give up everything it wants, or perhaps even get completely annihilated. Since the profound transformations that occur on the spiritual path usually seem to be a big problem to the ego, we shouldn't be surprised that it often puts up a lot of resistance.

Think about the ego as you would an adopted a child who never had a family and was just living on the streets. What does she need in order to turn into a happy human being who is a real benefit to the world? She needs love. She doesn't need to be beaten, right? You wouldn't adopt someone from an orphanage where she was never touched or loved, and try to solve her problems by yelling at her and abusing her. That's not going to turn her into a good person. A lot of times, when we first come to meditation, we think we have to discipline ourselves really strictly. But trying to be a stern taskmaster doesn't really work that well for most people. The ego will rebel. Of course, a kind of stern toughness is needed at times, and may be skillful then; keeping with the re-parenting metaphor, boundary setting and firmness are required sometimes.

What heals, matures, and eventually liberates the ego is, however, the ability to be present with awareness and compassion. We may not realize it, but it takes an enormous amount of loving-kindness to work on the spiritual path. Loving-kindness for ourselves and for others is the lubricating oil that allows us to change. It is loving-kindness that makes the journey enjoyable, and in fact, it is loving-kindness that makes it possible in the first place.

As we work in this way, the ego becomes more and more translucent, and its pure awakened essence, its buddha nature, shows through. But the ego never really goes away. It's a part of every human being, like our arms and legs. But as it becomes more transparent and clear, it no longer has to be the little kid running the universe with a huge load on his shoulders. The ego can relax and enjoy things rather than be the boss. The suchness—what's called *dharmata* in Sanskrit and sometimes "pure being" in English—can just be there. And with this transparency and loving-kindness, a basic shift from identifying with the illusory ego consciousness into awareness itself starts to happen.

Vajrayana Practice

As we have seen, the ultimate goal of all Buddhism is to help us uncover our buddha or awakened nature and to bring awareness to what's going on with our selves and our world. Of course, some people spontaneously awaken right out of the blue, but most of us need a lot more—a kind of step-by-step method and practice. The Vajrayana tradition has literally thousands of different practices, so if you are going to follow that path it is important to work with a teacher to help you chart the course that is best for you. You need a living relationship that forms a circle between the teacher and student to help you through the process of awakening and to show you a living example of the awakened mind. If the connection is auspicious, then that student-teacher relationship can be incredibly valuable.

Because the path of Vajrayana Buddhism is so vast, there is a lot of room to do whatever kind of practice you are drawn to. There are extensive long-term programs that transmit a whole body of practices and give the students a very thorough kind of training. At the same time, it's possible to attain awakening by just doing one practice for an entire lifetime. So it's best to sit down with your teacher and figure out what works for you. With so many practices to choose from, you are likely to need her help to find the ones that speak to your own heart. If you are in a comprehensive training program, then it also is important to work with a teacher to help navigate the spiritual and psychological territory.

In the beginning, it is necessary to achieve some level of mastery over our minds. If we don't, our thoughts will either throw us all over the place or settle into their old pathways and just run their habitual patterns. We need to be the masters of our thoughts, not vice versa, and the way we do that is to learn to bring the mind to shamatha, that is, to calm abiding or concentration. Unless we can, it doesn't matter what spiritual path we are following; whether it's Buddhism or something else, we won't really make much progress.

It may not seem like it, but just bringing the mind to rest actually takes a great deal of practice. If we work at it, however, we can learn to bring our mind to peace wherever we are, whatever is happening. The most common place to start is with meditation on the breath. Rather than following the breath, I prefer to cultivate a sense of joining awareness with the breath, so that you don't feel like you are watching it from the outside, but rather that you're experiencing it fully and completely without any separation. You don't need to control your breath or do any kind of breathing exercises; you just let yourself breathe naturally in whatever way feels right and spontaneous. Then at the same time, you try to become more and more aware of each instant of the breath as it rises and falls. The Tibetan word for meditation means to accustom ourselves. We're accustoming ourselves to focusing our mind and resting in our primordial purity.

Of course, there are scores of other practices aside from meditation on the breath. There is the practice of service, working for the benefit of others. There are rituals and chanting practices, yogic exercises and meditations that involve visualizing a whole mandala of awakened beings with an enlightened version of yourself in the middle. Then there is scholarship and study. All the different kinds of practices work on us in different ways. Some help us to be in touch on a body level, some on a heart level, and others on a mind level, and usually they work on all three together. There is, however, a catch. Because the methods of Vajrayana tend to be extremely powerful, it's necessary to think about what's safe, and that's why we usually work with the heart center first, last, and in between. The idea is that once the heart gets activated, it pervades all the practice. If that isn't happening, then there's a big problem. If we do these practices without an open heart and a lot of compassion, they are likely to backfire and produce harmful consequences. Of course, nothing is ever foolproof. But we need to sincerely practice expanding our loving-kindness, compassion, and generosity.

Although the spiritual path can be full of bliss and happiness, it isn't usually like that. At various points along the way, we are bound to collide with all the most difficult and painful things inside ourselves. But if we persevere, our practice will help purify us, help us release old thoughts and strategies, and help us come to calm abiding. It can help us deal skillfully with our habitual patterns and conflicted emotions, such as anger, fear, jealousy, hatred, pride, or arrogance, so that we can transform them into their original state of pure wisdom. Ultimately, all these practices help us clear away the ore that obscures the pure gold of our true buddha nature.

Vajrayana shares many of its practices with the other Buddhist traditions. We all practice service to others, chanting, group rituals, and shamatha and vipassana meditation. However, yidam meditation, in which we visualize ourselves in an enlightened mandala relating to and eventually becoming an enlightened being, is unique to Vajrayana, and so it deserves some special attention here.

Yidam is often translated as "deity" in English, but that word doesn't have the right feel to it. "Deity" sounds like some kind of Olympian god, and that's not what we're talking about. It would be more accurate to call them "awakened beings," because they are the activity aspect, arising out of compassion from awakened mind. But I think it is best to use the Tibetan term "yidam" since it carries less baggage than any of its English equivalents.

The yidam mandala we imagine in this practice is a symbolic representation of our own universe. All the phenomena of our lives are the phenomena of the mandala, and we are the yidam at its center. The yidam mandala is an awake manifestation of the divine energies of our mind in form, color, sound, and thought. In the mandala we unconsciously create in our everyday life, those enlightened energies are often obscured, so they appear in a distorted way. We enter into yidam practice to loosen our identification with those old distortions and habitual patterns. While doing this kind of practice, we try to rest in the true nature of mind—complete openness and emptiness that is at the same time clear, luminous, and aware. This practice helps us realize that state more fully by entering into and interacting with an awakened mandala that we create, and eventually by coming to see ourselves and all other beings as awakened beings, as the yidam.

When we get to the point in our practice that our body becomes the body of the yidam, we think of ourselves as a being of light, appearing inseparable with emptiness—which in fact is actually our situation all the time. This practice trains us to recognize that fact and to stop identifying with the small self or ego consciousness, our deluded sense of self, so we can come fully into our awakened identity. This transformation of identity is a huge part of yidam practice. In fact, in some ways the transformation of our limited, obscured self-identity is the core of the whole thing.

It's said that if we meditate in this way, all our obstacles will be removed and the *siddhis*, the accomplishments and the awakened activities, will naturally manifest themselves. At the same time, however, everything that isn't awakened mind comes to the surface and stares us in the face. When we're doing this kind of practice intensely, we may come to see the depth of the full catastrophe of our human mind. Eventually all our neurotic habit patterns—our depression, fear, and anxiety—get flushed to the surface and released out. But as they're flushed out, we reexperience their primal energy. Say for example, we have had some kind of very traumatic experience that we have repressed. As it comes back into consciousness and is experienced, it can be quite disturbing because it will feel like the trauma is happening all over again. But actually nothing is going on except that old energy is coming to the surface and being released. So we have to keep remembering that our neurotic habit patterns are not who we truly are, but only old energy from the past.

On the path of practice, we have to tolerate those old repressed energies as they come out and recognize the very deep fixations that we've had. They feel very real as they are being flushed out, but if we get engaged with them again, we just hinder the process of release. On the other hand, if we can experience that energy as the union of clarity and emptiness, it can very easily liberate itself. When we work with pride, for example, and allow it to liberate itself in this way, it turns into what's called the wisdom of equanimity, a very deep recognition of the equality of ourselves and all sentient beings. This is the process of refining the ore of our experience and separating out the obscuring elements to reveal the pure gold of our intrinsic buddha nature.

This process actually has an effect on what we call the subtle body as well as on the mind. The subtle body is a kind of energy system that mediates between our gross physical body and the very subtle realm of our pure awareness. Western science and medicine are largely unaware of the existence of the subtle body, but working with it is central to medical and yogic practice throughout Asia. The energy winds of the subtle body are called *lung* in Tibetan and *prana* in Sanskrit, and they circulate through the body in a vast network of channels that intersect in various key points in the body known as *chakras*. The *bindu* (in Tibetan, *tigli*) are drops of subtle energy that might be called our vital essences. Everything that makes up our energy body is the union of the prana, the channels, and the bindu. The further we get into yidam practice the more we work with the channels and the chakras. As we flush out the energy of our neurotic habit patterns, we remove the obstructions that bind our prana and prevent it from flowing properly.

But as I mentioned before, the methods of Vajrayana are extremely powerful, and we have to think about what's safe. In the beginning practices, we usually start working to open the heart chakra. Once we open our heart, true compassion for ourselves and others pervades all our practice, and if we don't do that, we will encounter all kinds of obstacles.

When we fully dedicate ourselves to yidam practice, many things happen to us psychologically, physically, and with the subtle body that are very hard to explain to someone who hasn't yet experienced them. The commentaries don't go into much of a description about what is actually happening. Much more of this kind of information is present in biographies of great yogis, yoginis, and sages. Conversations with our teacher(s) can help if they have traversed this territory before we have. Also, there is a self-revealing aspect of practice. As we do yidam practices over time, insights come, and we come to understand more and more deeply the great wisdom these practices embody, and the way we are being transformed and liberated will naturally, over time, reveal itself to us in our own experience.

Envisioning Tara

In Vajrayana we practice with a vast array of yidams, but Tara has a special kind of traction here in the West today. I am constantly amazed by how deeply she resonates even with those who have no real background or interest in Buddhism at all. I think there is a deep hunger for the wisdom of the divine feminine and a need to get the masculine and feminine energies of our culture into harmony and balance.

Traditionally, we in the West haven't really had an archetype of the awakened feminine that embodies both wisdom and sexuality, nurturing love and fierce love. In the Western religious tradition, the awakened feminine is most clearly embodied by Mary, the mother of Jesus. She is seen as the pure Madonna, but she's not allowed to be sexual. She had to conceive Jesus nonsexually, because in the West sex is often seen as gross or sinful. Jungian psychologists have found that there are two key archetypes of the feminine in the collective unconscious of our culture: the Madonna, who is pure, maternal, and wise; and the Whore, who is sensual and corrupt. But it is not just a matter of sexuality; the idea that spiritual women not only have wisdom, but a fierce, wrathful inner power, doesn't go over very well in the West either. This kind of split didn't exist in the pre-Christian goddess traditions of the West, but at some point, the patriarchy stamped out the full vision of the divine feminine, and there is a deep collective longing to have it back.

In Hinduism, the feminine is seen as *shakti*, the primordial cosmic energy of creation, while Vajrayana emphasizes the vast openness of the feminine. The feminine is seen as the womb of the divine mother that holds us all. Without space, without emptiness, nothing would be able to exist. Her emptiness holds all of us in divine love, nourishes us, gives us life, and sustains us. This wisdom of emptiness is therefore personified as Tara, Prajnaparamita (the great goddess we encountered in the sutras of the second turning), and other awakened female beings. The awakened feminine is said to be the mother of all the buddhas, because it is the realization of emptiness or openness—nonconceptual and nondual—that brings us to awakening. Indeed, wisdom is itself the essence of the divine feminine in Buddhist tantra.

In her aspect as divine mother, Tara nurtures all life and gives birth to the awakened ones, but she also manifests a fierce power that cuts through our problems and obscurations, and most especially through our deep-rooted ignorance. She is like our Mother Earth who supplies us with everything we need, but can also manifest earthquakes, hurricanes, tidal waves, and tornados. The divine mother is a compassionate loving presence who's always available to us, but she may display a terrifying ferocity if that is what we need in order to wake up.

Coming to abide in the realization of *shunyata*, the inherent openness and emptiness of all phenomenon that is Tara's essence, is what gives birth to awakening. But we have to be careful with the word "emptiness," because it gives a kind of desolate and depressing feeling to a lot of people here in the West. It is important to realize that emptiness is not just blankness; it has a fertile womb-like quality that provides everything needed to allow us to grow and for all things to manifest. If we see clearly, we realize that all appearance is appearance-emptiness, that all awareness is awareness-emptiness. Suzuki Roshi, the founder of the San Francisco Zen Center, once said that resting in emptiness is like sucking at the breast of the mother. When we are actually resting in the union of emptiness and appearance that is our true nature, there is a feeling of complete and total fulfillment, and we instinctively know that there is nothing we lack.

As we engage in this practice, we come to know Tara and develop a profound appreciation for the way she works in our lives. But it's not usually an instantaneous process. It takes time before we feel we have a real relationship with her. Just as in our daily lives, we might meet somebody we really like, but developing a relationship with them requires love and dedication. We have to put in the energy to meet with that person, to visit with them and get to know them. Meditating on Tara works in the same way. We may have very powerful experiences in the beginning, but they may also come in the middle or the end or at any time along the way. As we get to know Tara and receive her blessings, we come to see that she is a reflection of our own true nature. She reflects all of the aspects of the awakened feminine. She is the beautiful, all-compassionate, all-loving mother. She is the embodiment of peace, generosity, and all the other perfections.

Tara's special activity, especially in her green form, is to remove fears and obstacles and to help create all the supportive conditions needed for our awakening. In fact, in Tibetan one of her names means "She Who Liberates" or "She Who Ferries Beings Across The Ocean of Samsara." She has the power to help destroy, release, and alleviate all of our difficulties both internally and externally. She performs four specific kinds of "awakened activities." The first one is pacification. This includes meditation, resolving conflicts, soothing, calming, and bringing peace. The next one is enriching. This is a kind of nourishment like giving food, water, encouragement, teachings, or knowledge, or providing whatever else is needed for people to be healthy and to grow and prosper. The third enlightened activity, magnetizing, brings together whatever is needed in a particular situation. Tara might, for example, bring various people together who could benefit from the Dharma teachings. The last of her enlightened activities, destroying, may sound harmful, but it actually has to do with setting limits, creating boundaries, and stopping things or relationships that have outlived their usefulness and need to come to an end. It is fierce activity or active compassion.

On a personal level, this practice helps us recognize that we have all Tara's awakened qualities and the potential for all her awakened activities in ourselves. Along with the formal sitting practice, we allow the enlightened qualities to flourish within ourselves, so that whatever is needed in any given situation, for ourselves or others, can spontaneously manifest out of us. If a situation calls for a pacifying influence, for calming people or bringing them together, then that kind of activity will spontaneously arise. If the situation needs some enriching, perhaps we need to study certain Dharma teachings or engage in furthering our own education so that our innate intelligence can manifest. The same is true for magnetizing people together or for the more fierce energy of destruction where new boundaries have to be set or old patterns ended.

It doesn't matter if you are a woman or a man; the more you practice Tara, the more you come to embody her enlightened qualities, and
the more you become an emanation of Tara in the world. In Buddhist
tantra, we sometimes meditate ourselves as male yidams, sometimes as
female yidams, and sometimes as the union of the male and female. All
of us have male and female aspects within ourselves. It's said that in the
subtle energy body, all of the bindu, our drops of vital energy, are the
union of the female and male buddhas. That's why we practice to purify,
transform and liberate the masculine and feminine within us, and ultimately to bring them into complete union. In fact, emptiness and form,
heaven and earth, female and male—all seeming dualities must be seen
in their underlying unity to fully realize our true nature. All dualities are
inseparable, and in their final essence they are all wisdom and compassion united. So as we practice, it doesn't matter whether we're female or
male in our bodies. What matters is that we do the right practice for us
and for the world.

Whatever our gender, as we practice we come to understand how
Tara manifests in all her various forms and activities. We open up the
awakened feminine within us and allow the full range of awakened
qualities to come to fruition. But this is not the restricted Western version of femininity. Tara is not just quiet and demure, sitting with her legs
crossed all the time. As we have seen, she has countless other aspects
and qualities as well. She can be wise, sexy, fierce, pacifying, beautiful, and confrontational. But this doesn't mean we should neglect our
masculine qualities either, because our practice opens those up too. In
our tradition, we often meditate on ourselves as Chakrasamvara, who
embodies the clarity, strength, and skill in means of the masculine
principle. Cultivating a relationship with Tara and the other yidams
helps bring us into the true balance of female and male. But at the
same time, we are getting to know someone we can call on anytime we
need help.

In order to do Tara practice correctly, you need to work with a teacher
that you feel connected to. But along with Avalokiteshvara (Chenrezig
in Tibetan), the bodhisattva who hears the cries of the world, Tara is

considered to be one of the safest yidams to work with. So it is all right to experiment with a simple form of Tara practice on your own.

Like any tantric practice, you begin by taking a comfortable posture, settling your mind calmly, and declaring your intention to take refuge in the Three Jewels—the Buddha, the Dharma, and the Sangha. We also remember that we are not doing meditation just for ourselves, but to awaken in order to benefit all beings. Then out of emptiness, you visualize the seed syllable *Tam* appearing in the sky in front of you. If you know what the Tibetan character for Tam looks like you can visualize that; if not, use the English spelling. Then from that Tam, imagine Tara instantly appears, sitting on a full open lotus and a flat disk of the moon. She is radiantly beautiful and serene. Her skin is blue-green like the color of a mountain lake, and she is arrayed in silks and jewels, symbolizing both her complete integration of the six perfections, and her full awakening as a completely realized buddha.

Next, imagine that you are radiating light from your heart to purify the phenomenal world and make offerings to the enlightened ones. Then invite Tara's supreme wisdom to be present with you. Visualize this wisdom raining down on you from the heavens in the form of countless small Taras. While you do this, visualize that these imagined Taras are inseparable from her true wisdom. Think that the minds of all your spiritual teachers and of all those who have shown you love and compassion are united with her, and that she is now truly present in the sky in front of you. It is okay if your visualization isn't very clear or strong at first; the important thing is to feel her loving presence.

She is the mother of all the buddhas, the essence of compassion in action. Her right foot is slightly extended, because she is ready to leap to the aid of beings. Her right hand is opened out and is resting on her right knee in the gesture, or *mudra*, of generosity. Her left hand holds the stem of a beautiful lotus flower that is blossoming next to her left ear. Begin repeating her mantra, *Om Taré Tu Taré Turé So Ha*, and try to generate true devotion and love for her. Then visualize that a river of nectar, or *amrita*—liquid light turquoise green in color—comes from her outstretched right hand into you, entering either through the heart or crown of the head. This river of amrita removes all fear, gives protection, clears away obstacles and obscurations, and transmits enlightened awareness into you and all beings. Then make prayers to Tara, while receiving her blessing.

Next you see Tara dissolve into light and merge into you. Think that your mind is inseparable with Tara's mind and with all enlightened minds everywhere. In the culmination of the meditation, you imagine yourself as actually being Tara, appearing as a body made of light that is inseparable from emptiness, emptiness that is inseparable from her form. Imagine the blue-green seed syllable *Tam* resting in your heart. From this seed syllable light radiates out to all beings, sending joy, compassion, loving-kindness, strength, equanimity, and all the other blissful qualities of the enlightened beings. Keep repeating the mantra over and over again as you imagine this.

When you are done, you gradually dissolve the visualization into a drop of turquoise-green light in the heart area. This radiates brilliantly: the essence of your true nature. Finally, this brilliant drop dissolves into space, like a rainbow disappearing into the sky. Rest your mind naturally in tranquil meditation for a few minutes more or longer if you feel like it. For this part of the meditation you should have your eyes open, if they weren't already. Finally, as we do at the end of all our meditation practices, after seeing ourselves and all beings re-arise as Tara, we dedicate any and all merit of this practice to help bring all living beings everywhere to liberation, complete freedom from suffering.

In this way Tara practice, like all Vajrayana, uses duality to help us realize the complete emptiness of our dualistic thinking. It uses our sense of being separate from the divine, from our own awakening, to dismantle that separation and with it our deluded perception of the world. When we first call on Tara, we envision her as an awakened being separate from ourselves, but the more we interact with her, the more we come to dismantle that very separation. We eventually come to see that we are completely inseparable from her and her enlightened mind, and with that realization a profound shift in identity occurs. The pure gold of our true nature shines forth, and we become an enlightened yidam and the world our sacred mandala.

7

The Buddha's Dream

Existence is beyond the power of words
To define:
Terms may be used
But none of them are absolute
—LAO TZU[102]

Each turning of the wheel was an invitation from the Buddha—an invitation to break out of the claustrophobic cocoon of our thoughts, ideas, and beliefs, and to experience the mystery of things just as they are. These teachings are the exact opposite of the bedtime stories your parents used to tell you to put you to sleep at night. They are stories that invite you to wake up and realize you have been dreaming.

As we continue to turn the wheel of Dharma amid the bewildering complexities of the twenty-first-century world, it is vital that we understand the treasury of wisdom the Buddha left us in the great sutras of the three turnings. But we must not confuse the Buddha's beautiful teachings with the ungraspable mystery to which they point. As we weave our own stories from the threads of the great classical teachings and our own culture and experience, we must heed the Buddha's warning not to be seduced into believing in those dreams.

No matter what our beliefs or values, this is a warning the modern world desperately needs to hear. How are we to live in harmony on this small, divided planet when we believe that the views of our own community or our own subculture are the only ones derived from true mystical experience, incontrovertible scientific evidence, or the infallible word of God? In a world of global interdependence and instant communication, the idea that our own way of looking at things is the one true way is fast becoming a luxury we can no longer afford.

Yet it is easy to take this insight into the emptiness of our thoughts too far. Even though our dreams may not be real, *it matters what we dream.* Compare the dreams of Pol Pot, who believed that exterminating the millions who opposed him would allow the creation of a great agrarian utopia in Cambodia, and those of the Dalai Lama, who believes that he must foster love and compassion for all—even the Chinese invaders who threatened to destroy the culture of his homeland. They are both just dreams, but would anyone say that it makes no difference which of those fills our hearts and minds? Pol Pot's fantasy of personal grandeur and a great unstained utopia led step by step to the killing fields of Cambodia, piled high with the corpses of his countrymen. The Dalai Lama's vision of kindness and compassion continues to inspire countless people around the world and promote their spiritual growth and well-being.

But it is not enough that our dreams be wholesome. They must also be in harmony with the world, or they may still lead us into the abyss. Pol Pot's vision of an agrarian utopia was, in its way, a beautiful dream, but it could never tolerate the imperfections of human life. And we all know that even actions motivated by the most sincere desire to help can cause horrible problems if they are rooted in delusion. So once we have developed mental stability through our meditation practice, we need to examine our old habitual dreams with a fearless objectivity in order to find out if they are actually in accord with the reality of things and whether they produce happiness or suffering.

The New Buddhism and the Old

When you read, contemplate, and practice the wisdom of the great sutras, you are connecting to the deepest roots of the Buddhist tradition. There are no Buddhist teachings more classic or profound than those found in these great sutras, and none that point more clearly to the timeless awareness that lies beyond all words and all teachings. At the same time, however, our cultural perspective and our personal experiences are so different from those of the yogis of ancient India or of the traditional Buddhist commentators of Asia that we can hardly expect our conceptual understanding to be the same as theirs.

Indeed, the mere fact that average laypeople would ever study and practice the sutras represents a radical break with the past. Traditionally, such things were the purview of small groups of monks who dedicated their entire lives to the Buddhist path. Things began to change in the nineteenth century as Asian Buddhism came under increasing pressure from Western colonialism, Western religion, and Western secularism, and some of its most progressive leaders realized that they needed to spread those teachings and practices more widely if they were to survive the onslaught of the modern world. But the real break came when Buddhism leaped from the traditional agrarian societies of Asia into the cauldron of consumer capitalism, and Buddhism's sophisticated philosophy and vast array of meditation practices were thrown open to all comers. The result has been something chaotic, confusing, and to my mind at least, wonderful. Understandably, traditionalists worry that something deep and profound is being lost amid the banalities of consumer culture and pop psychology. But the world is changing in a profound and irreversible way, and Buddhism too must change if it is to survive.

The same thing, however, can be said of contemporary society itself. Science has given us unimaginable new powers but not the wisdom to know how to use them. Our greed has led us to the brink of an unprecedented environmental crisis, and our ancient hatreds are being transformed into a threat to our very survival as the means of mass destruction spread to the farthest corners of the globe. Yet we are so mired in delusion that we seem incapable of taking action or recognizing the hollow void that lies at the heart of our relentless quest for wealth and the power it brings. Day by day, year by year, it seems increasingly clear that the postmodern world is heading for a crisis point: we must either change our ways or face the devastating consequences.

The explosion of interest in meditation and mindfulness in recent times is no accident. It is part of the growing recognition of this desperate need for change, and it shows us that the ancient remedies Buddhism offers for our greed, hate, and delusion have never been more relevant or timely. But as this new, more secular form of Dharma spreads, so does the danger that we will lose sight of the tradition's deepest, most profound teachings. Admittedly, the study of the great sutras is something of an acquired taste, but there is no better way to assure that the new Buddhism doesn't turn into a shallow imitation of the old, and that the deepest wisdom of the Buddha does indeed take root in the postmodern world.

The Path

Studying the sutras is not like learning algebra. The wisdom they contain is so deep and profound that it literally has no end. The more effort you put into your studies, the more you get out of it. And even though it may not seem like it at first, the more you actualize those teachings in yourself, the more the world will reap the benefits.

But studying the sutras is not enough. Sooner or later we have to take whatever intellectual understanding we have gained and put it into practice if we are to experience the reality to which the teachings point. Acting with virtue and compassion is the foundation for the entire spiritual journey, and we need to bring our mindful attention to our motivations and purify our behavior as best we can, if we are to make any lasting progress on the way. Then with that as our foundation, we need to take our understanding onto the meditation cushion. By alternating back and forth between meditation practice and study and reflection, the real meaning of the teachings can penetrate to deeper and deeper levels of our being, and we will indeed come to "taste the truth of the Buddha's words" as our clarity, insight, and love grow.

This journey through the wisdom of the great sutras we have begun can be a lifetime adventure leading us to endless new discoveries and ever-deepening realization. The teachings of Buddha may be just dreams woven of words and concepts, but they are supremely wholesome dreams, dreams that are in tune with the way things truly are. If we can go beyond the mere words the Buddha spoke and taste their true meaning, they point directly to the shores of liberation that lie beyond our sea of dreams. So I invite you to join me in this dream and see what happens to your life and to the world we share.

Notes

1. See for example, Mu Soeng, *Heart Sutra: Ancient Buddhist Wisdom in the Light of Quantum Reality* (Cumberland, RI: Primary Point Press, 1991).

2. The Sarvastidavan school of early Buddhism recorded its canon in Sanskrit, and although much of the original was lost, most of it survives in Chinese and Tibetan translations. Although there are some important differences from the Theravadan canon recorded in Pali, they are generally quite similar.

3. No copies of this sutra in the original Sanskrit are known to have survived, but there are five whole or partial Chinese translations and one in Tibetan. One translation from the Tibetan has been published in English and two from Chinese. John Powers (trans.), *The Wisdom of Buddha: The Samdhinirmocana Mahayana Sutra* (Berkeley, CA: Dharma Publishing, 1995); Thomas Cleary (trans.), *Buddhist Yoga: A Comprehensive Course* (Boston: Shambhala, 1995); John P. Keenan (trans.), *The Scripture on the Explication of Underlying Meaning* (Berkeley, CA: Numata Center for Buddhist Translation and Research, 2000).

4. See note 35 for a discussion of the arguments about the order in which the sutras were written.

5. There are numerous English translations of most of these sutras. Some of the quotations in the book come directly from a particular translation; those are indicated with a footnote. Sometimes, however, the meaning could be made more clear by working different translations together into a new version, and those passages will not be footnoted.

6. For a wide-ranging and nuanced examination of the Axial Age, see Robert Bellah, *Religion in Human Evolution: From the Paleolithic to the Axial Age* (Cambridge, MA: Belknap Press, 2011).

7. Samyutta Nikaya 56, 11. Bhikkhu Bodhi, trans., *The Connected Discourses of the Buddha: A Translation of the Samyutta Nikaya* (Somerville, MA: Wisdom Publications, 2000), 1844.

8. Ibid.

9. Ibid.

10. Ibid.

11. Ibid.

12. Majjhima Nikaya 122. Bhikkhu Nanamoli and Bhikkhu Bodhi, trans., *The Middle Length Discourses of the Buddha: A Translation of the Majjhima Nikaya* (Boston: Wisdom Publications, 2001), 975.

13. Khuddaka Nikaya, Udana 8.3. Thanissaro Bhikkhu, "Udana: Exclamations," (free pdf, 2012), 113, http://www.accesstoinsight.org/lib/authors/thanissaro/udana.pdf.

14. Samyutta Nikaya 56, 11. Bodhi, *The Connected Discourses of the Buddha*, 1844.

15. Anguttara Nikaya 10:216. Bhikkhu Bodhi, trans., *The Numerical Discourses of the Buddha: A Translation of the Anguttara Nikaya* (Boston: Wisdom Publications, 2012), 1535.

16. Dhammapada, v. 183, quoted in Bhikkhu Bodhi, *The Noble Eightfold Path: The Way to the End of Suffering* (Kandy, Sri Lanka: Buddhist Publication Society, 2010), 48.

17. Thich Nhat Hanh, *For a Future to Be Possible: Commentaries on the Five Mindfulness Trainings* (Berkeley, CA: Parallax Press, 1993).

18. Ibid.

19. Bodhi, *The Noble Eightfold Path*, 65–66.

20. For example, in Majjhima Nikaya 4. In Nanamoli and Bodhi, *The Middle Length Discourses of the Buddha*, this is pages 102–7.

21. For a good summary of this path see Nanamoli and Bodhi, *The Middle Length Discourses of the Buddha*, 34–41.

22. Majjhima Nikaya 51.

23. Majjhima Nikaya 51. Nanamoli and Bodhi, *The Middle Length Discourses of the Buddha*, 448.

24. Ibid., 450–51.

25. Majjhima Nikaya 4. Nanamoli and Bodhi, *The Middle Length Discourses of the Buddha*, 106.

26. Ibid.

27. Ibid.

28. Majjhima Nikaya 10. Nanamoli and Bodhi, *The Middle Length Discourses of the Buddha*. In the Pali version of this sutra, it is somewhat unclear if the practitioner is practicing vipassana or shamatha when following the breath, but in the Sarvastivadan version, which was originally in Sanskrit, the practitioner does appear to start with shamatha. See Thich Nhat Hanh, *Awakening of the Heart: Essential Buddhist Sutras and Commentaries,* (Berkeley, CA: Parallax Press, 2012) 197, 198.

29. Nanamoli and Bodhi, *The Middle Length Discourses of the Buddha*, 40.

30. Karl Brunnholzl, *The Heart Attack Sutra: A New Commentary on the Heart Sutra* (Ithaca, NY: Snow Lion, 2012).

31. Gregory Schopen, *Figments and Fragments of Mahayana Buddhism in India* (Honolulu: University of Hawai'i Press, 2005) 15.

32. See Schopen, *Figments and Fragments of Mahayana Buddhism in India*, 3–24.

33. See Red Pine, *The Heart Sutra: Translation and Commentary* (Berkeley, CA: Counterpoint, 2004), 29–32.

34. Lex Hixon, *Mother of the Buddhas: Meditation on the Prajnaparamita Sutra* (Wheaton, IL: The Theosophical Publishing House, 1993), 95–96.

35. Although the pioneering Western scholar Edward Conze argued that the *Perfection of Wisdom in 8,000 Lines* was the first of the prajnaparamita sutras and that the *Diamond Sutra* dated from a far later era, there is convincing evidence to give the *Diamond Sutra* the title as the oldest prajnaparamita sutra. The Chinese were far more meticulous historians than the Indians, and Conze based his chronology on the order in which the prajnaparamita sutras were first translated into Chinese. However, there is no particular reason to assume that these texts were translated in the same order in which they were first recorded. The first translation of the *Perfection of Wisdom in 8,000 Lines* into Chinese was in the second century of the common era, and even Conze dated the original text to the first century BCE. Scholars in Japan and elsewhere in Asia have relied on content analysis for their chronology and have generally concluded the *Diamond Sutra* to be the most ancient. In the West, many contemporary scholars including Gregory Schopen (*Figments and Fragments of Mahayana*

Buddhism in India, 31–32) have reached similar conclusions. His linguistic analysis indicates that parts of the *Perfection of Wisdom in 8,000 Lines* were an elaboration of the themes originally presented in a more oral style in the *Diamond Sutra.* Others point out that the questions in the *Diamond Sutra* are put directly to the Buddha by his disciple Subhuti, while in the *Perfection of Wisdom in 8,000 Lines* Subhuti answers the questions, and logically it would appear that the sutra in which Subhuti learns about the perfection of wisdom would have to precede the sutras in which he teaches it. Thich Nhat Hanh argues that because the beginning of the *Diamond Sutra* says the Buddha gave his teachings to an audience of 1,250 monks but does not mention the presence of any bodhisattvas as other prajnaparamita sutras do, that it must have been addressed to the Buddha's earliest followers. (It should be noted, however, that some of the Chinese translations do include a mention of bodhisattvas in the audience. On this point see Red Pine, *The Heart Sutra,* 47.) It is also interesting that the *Diamond Sutra* never uses the term "emptiness," which is so important in the rest of the prajnaparamita literature, which might indicate that the sutra predates the popularity of the term.

36. Red Pine, *The Diamond Sutra: Text and Commentaries Translated from Sanskrit and Chinese* (Berkeley, CA: Counterpoint, 2001), 2–3.

37. Ibid., 3.

38. Thich Nhat Hanh, *Chanting from the Heart,* rev. ed. (Berkeley, CA: Parallax Press, 2006), 339.

39. Red Pine, *The Heart Sutra,* 21; Hajime Nakamura, *Indian Buddhism: A Survey with Bibliographic Notes* (New Delhi: Motilal Banarsidass, 1987), 160; Edward Conze, *The Prajnaparamita Literature* (The Hague: Mouton, 1960), 9; Jan Nattier, "The Heart Sutra: A Chinese Apocryphal Text," *Journal of the International Association of Buddhist Studies* 15, no. 2 (1992), 153–223.

40. Some versions of the sutra include an introduction in which the Buddha gives Avalokiteshvara the power to make his realization, and a conclusion in which the Buddha endorses Avalokiteshvara's conclusions. But most scholars believe these sections are a later addition intended to give the text greater credibility and were not in the original.

41. Most English translations say that because the bodhisattvas have ended all delusions they "attain" or "reach" final nirvana. But this is problematic, because Avalokiteshvara just got through saying that there is no attainment. Red Pine renders this passage, "They see through delusion and finally nirvana" (*The Heart Sutra*, 136), which makes much more sense to me. However, the other versions have become so standard in the West that I decided to use to a more ambiguous translation that can be read either way.

42. Ruth Fuller Sasaki, trans, *The Record of Linji*, ed. Thomas Yuho Kirchner (Honolulu, University of Hawai'i Press, 2009), 22.

43. See James William Coleman, *The New Buddhism: The Western Transformation of an Ancient Tradition* (New York: Oxford, 2001).

44. See Guy Newland, *The Two Truths: A Study of Madhyamika Philosophy as Presented in the Monastic Textbooks of the Ge-luk-ba Order of Tibetan Buddhism*, Doctoral Dissertation, Department of Religious Studies, University of Virginia, May 1988; *Appearance and Reality: The Two Truths in the Four Buddhist Tenet Systems* (Ithaca, NY: Snow Lion, 1999); Sonam Thakchoe, *The Two Truths Debate: Tsongkhapa and Gorampa on the Middle Way* (Boston: Wisdom, 2007).

45. See John Powers, "The Term 'Samdhinirmocana' in the Title of the Samdhinirmocana Sutra," *Studies in Central and East Asian Religions: Journal of the Seminar for Buddhist Studies*, Volume 4 (1992): 52–62.

46. Keenan, *The Scripture on the Explication of Underlying Meaning*, 11. There are three English translations of the *Sutra of the Explanation of the Profound Secrets*, two from Chinese and one from Tibetan—see note 3. I have switched back and forth freely between the three trying to find the words and phrases that would be easiest for a reader unskilled in technical Buddhist philosophy to understand.

47. Ibid.

48. Ibid.,12.

49. Ibid.

50. Cleary, *Buddhist Yoga*, 9.

51. Red Pine, *The Lankavatara Sutra: A Translation and Commentary*, (Berkeley, CA: Counterpoint, 2012), 220.

52. Ibid., 79.

53. For example: "Kaccayanagotta Sutta: To Kaccayana Gotta (on Right View)" (SN 12.15), translated from the Pali by Thanissaro Bhikkhu. Access to Insight (Legacy Edition), 30 November 2013, http://www.accesstoinsight .org/tipitaka/sn/sn12/sn12.015.than.html.

54. Keenan, *The Scripture on the Explication of Underlying Meaning*, 24.

55. Cleary, *Buddhist Yoga*, 9.

56. Ibid., 14.

57. Keenan, *The Scripture on the Explication of Underlying Meaning*, 23.

58. Powers, *The Wisdom of Buddha*, 69.

59. Ibid. 71.

60. Edward Conze, *Buddhism: Its Essence and Development* (Birmingham, UK: Windhorse Publications, 1951), 106.

61. See Paul J. Griffiths, *On Being Mindless: Buddhist Meditation and the Mind-Body Problem* (La Salle, IL: Open Court Publishing, 1986).

62. Powers, *The Wisdom of Buddha*, 71.

63. Red Pine, *The Lankavatara Sutra*, 75.

64. Powers, *The Wisdom of Buddha*, 77.

65. Ibid., 81.

66. Ibid.

67. Keenan, *The Scripture on the Explication of Underlying Meaning*, 31.

68. Powers, *The Wisdom of Buddha*, 83.

69. Ibid.

70. Ibid., 87.

71. This and the following three quotations are from William H. Grosnick, trans., "The *Tathagatagarbha Sutra*," in *Buddhism in Practice*, ed. Donald S. Lopez, (Princeton University Press, 1995), 94–104.

72. Diana Y. Paul, trans., *The Sutra of Queen Simala of the Lion's Roar* (Berkeley, CA: Numata Center for Buddhist Translation, 2004), 25.

73. Ibid., 52.

74. Ibid., 53.

75. Red Pine, *Lankavatara Sutra*, 241.

76. Arya Maitreya, *Buddha Nature: The Mahayana Uttaratantra Shastra*, Rosemarie Fuchs, trans. (Ithaca, NY: Snow Lion Publications, 2000), 20.

77. See Schopen, *Figments and Fragments of Mahayana Buddhism in India*, 3–24.

78. Keenan, *The Scripture on the Explication of Underlying Meaning,* 40–41.

79. Powers, *The Wisdom of Buddha,* 113.

80. The Pali Canon contains a slightly different list of the perfections, but they are generally not given as much attention as they are in the Mahayana traditions.

81. Powers, *The Wisdom of Buddha,* 153.

82. Ibid., 157.

83. Conze, *Buddhism,* 106.

84. William James, *Psychology: The Briefer Course* (Notre Dame, IN: Notre Dame University Press, 1985), 26.

85. Powers, *The Wisdom of Buddha,* 69.

86. Buddhist psychology usually includes the "mind consciousness" as a sixth sense consciousness, but in this passage they are listed independently. Later Buddhist thought typically divides the psyche into eight consciousnesses, not the seven mentioned in this sutra, by separating the "thinking mind" into the "mind consciousness" (*mano vijnana*) that creates an image based on the sense consciousness and the "afflicted thinking" (*manas*) that clings to the idea of a self. However, the distinction between the two is not always clearly drawn, and for our purposes at least, it is easier to treat the two together.

87. See for example, David Kalupahana, *The Principles of Buddhist Psychology* (Albany: State University of New York Press, 1987), 137.

88. Keenan, *The Scripture on the Explication of Underlying Meaning,* 28.

89. Hsuan-tsang, "Demonstration of Consciousness Only," 7–372 in Francis H. Cook, trans., *Three Texts on Consciousness Only* (Berkeley, CA: Numata Center for Buddhist Translation and Research, 1999); Gareth Sparham (trans.), *Ocean of Eloquence: Tsong kha pa's Commentary on the Yogacara Doctrine of Mind* (Albany: State University of New York Press, 1993), 72.

90. Thich Nhat Hanh, *Transformation at the Base: Fifty Verses on the Nature of Consciousness* (Berkeley, CA: Parallax Press, 2001).

91. For example, early in his career Tsongkhapa, the founder of the Geluk school of Tibetan Buddhism, wrote a very insightful analysis of the nature of the alaya vijnana, but he eventually came to argue that it was a fictitious construct that was useful only as a heuristic device. See Sparham, *Ocean of Eloquence.* The current Dalai Lama (the most prominent member of

the Geluk school) continues to uphold this view in spite of the support the concept of the alaya vijnana appears to have from Western psychological thought. See Franscisco J. Varela, (ed.), *Sleeping, Dreaming, and Dying: An Exploration of Consciousness with the Dalai Lama* (Boston: Wisdom Publications, 1997), 86–88.

92. Cleary, *Buddhist Yoga*, 21.

93. James, *Psychology*, 38.

94. Keenan, *The Scripture on the Explication of Underlying Meaning*, 38.

95. Khenchen Thrangu Rinpoche, *Everyday Consciousness and Buddha-Awakening* (Ithaca, NY: Snow Lion Publications, 2002), 30.

96. George Herbert Mead, *Mind, Self, and Society* (University of Chicago Press, 1934), 178.

97. Vasubandhu, "Thirty Verses on Consciousness Only," trans. Ben Connelly and Weijen Teng, in *Inside Vasubandhu's Yogacara*, Ben Connelly (Somerville, MA, Wisdom Publications, 2016), 20.

98. Mead, 182.

99. The use of "the dream" and "the mystery" to describe the first two characteristics of phenomena originally came from some of the Zen priests who were studying the *Sutra of the Explanation of the Profound Secrets* under Anderson Roshi's guidance. The priests called the third characteristic "the reality," but Anderson Roshi prefers the "absence of the dream in the mystery," since it doesn't seem to privilege one of the three characteristics over the others. But the "absence of the dream in the mystery" is a bit too much of a mouthful, so I am using "the silence" here.

100. "Upajjhatthana Sutta: Subjects for Contemplation" (AN 5.57), translated from the Pali by Thanissaro Bhikkhu. *Access to Insight (Legacy Edition)*, 30 November 2013, http://www.accesstoinsight.org/tipitaka/an/an05/an05 .057.than.html. Accessed 11 August 2014.

101. Powers, *The Wisdom of Buddha*, 157.

102. Witter Bynner, trans., *The Way of Life According to Lao Tzu* (New York: Capricorn Books, 1962), 25. Originally published in 1944.

Bibliography

Anderson, Reb. *The Third Turning of the Wheel: Wisdom of the Samdhinirmocana Sutra*. Berkeley, CA: Rodmell, Press, 2012.

Bodhi, Bhikkhu. *The Noble Eightfold Path: The Way to the End of Suffering*. Kandy, Sri Lanka: Buddhist Publication Society, 2010.

Bodhi, Bhikkhu, trans. *The Connected Discourses of the Buddha: A Translation of the Samyutta Nikaya*. Somerville, MA: Wisdom Publications, 2000.

———. *The Middle Length Discourses of the Buddha: A Translation of the Majjhima Nikaya*. Boston: Wisdom Publications, 1995.

———. *The Numerical Discourses of the Buddha: A Translation of the Anguttara Nikaya*. Boston: Wisdom Publications, 2012

Brunnholzl, Karl. *The Heart Attack Sutra: A New Commentary on the Heart Sutra*. Ithaca, NY: Snow Lion, 2012.

Bynner, Witter, trans. *The Way of Life According to Lao Tzu*. New York: Capricorn Books, 1962.

Cleary, Thomas, trans. *Buddhist Yoga: A Comprehensive Course*. Boston: Shambhala, 1995.

Coleman, James William. *The New Buddhism: The Western Transformation of an Ancient Tradition*. New York: Oxford, 2001.

Connelly, Ben. *Inside Vasubandhu's Yogacara*. Somerville, MA: Wisdom Publications, 2016.

Conze, Edward. *Buddhism: Its Essence and Development*. Birmingham, UK: Windhorse Publications, 1951.

———. *The Prajnaparamita Literature*. The Hague: Mouton, 1960.

Cook, Francis H., trans. *Three Texts on Consciousness Only*. Berkeley, CA: Numata Center for Buddhist Translation and Research, 1999.

Bibliography

Cooley, Charles Horton. *Human Nature and the Social Order.* New York: Charles Scribner's Sons, 1902.

Freud, Sigmund. *New Introductory Lectures on Psychoanalysis.* Penguin Freud Library 2, 1933.

Fuller Sasaki, Ruth, trans. *The Record of Linji.* Edited by Thomas Yuho Kirchner. Honolulu: University of Hawai'i Press, 2009.

Griffiths, Paul J. *On Being Mindless: Buddhist Meditation and the Mind-Body Problem.* La Salle, IL: Open Court Publishing, 1986.

Grosnick, William H., trans. "The *Tathagatagarbha Sutra.*" In *Buddhism in Practice,* edited by Donald S. Lopez. Princeton University Press, 1995.

Hanh, Thich Nhat. *Awakening of the Heart: Essential Buddhist Sutras and Commentaries.* Berkeley, CA: Parallax Press, 2012.

———. *Chanting from the Heart.* Rev. ed. Berkeley, CA: Parallax Press, 2006.

———. *For a Future to Be Possible: Commentaries on the Five Mindfulness Trainings.* Berkeley, CA: Parallax Press, 1993.

———. *Transformation at the Base: Fifty Verses on the Nature of Consciousness.* Berkeley, CA: Parallax Press, 2001.

Hixon, Lex. *Mother of the Buddhas: Meditation on the Prajnaparamita Sutra.* Wheaton, IL: The Theosophical Publishing House, 1993.

James, William. *Psychology: The Briefer Course.* Notre Dame, IN: Notre Dame University Press, 1985.

Jung, Carl. *The Archetypes and the Collective Unconscious.* London: Routledge, 2006.

Kalupahana, David P. *The Principles of Buddhist Psychology.* Albany: State University of New York Press, 1987.

Keenan, John P., trans., *The Scripture on the Explication of Underlying Meaning.* Berkeley, CA: Numata Center for Buddhist Translation and Research, 2000.

Maitreya, Arya. *Buddha Nature: The Mahayana Uttaratantra Shastra.* Rosemarie Fuchs, trans. Ithaca, NY: Snow Lion Publications, 2000.

Mead, George Herbert. *Mind, Self, and Society.* Chicago: University of Chicago Press, 1934.

Nakamura, Hajime. *Indian Buddhism: A Survey with Bibliographic Notes.* New Delhi: Motilal Banarsidass, 1987.

Nanamoli, Bhikkhu, and Bhikkhu Bodhi, trans. *The Middle Length Discourses of the Buddha: A Translation of the Majjhima Nikaya.* Boston: Wisdom Publications, 2001.

Nattier, Jan. "The Heart Sutra: A Chinese Apocryphal Text." *Journal of the International Association of Buddhist Studies* 15, no. 2 (1992): 153–223.

Newland, Guy. *Appearance and Reality: The Two Truths in the Four Buddhist Tenet Systems.* Ithaca, NY: Snow Lion, 1999.

———. *The Two Truths: A Study of Madhyamika Philosophy as Presented in the Monastic Textbooks of the Ge-luk-ba Order of Tibetan Buddhism.* Doctoral Dissertation, Department of Religious Studies, University of Virginia, May 1988.

Paul, Diana Y., trans. *The Sutra of Queen Simala of the Lion's Roar.* Berkeley: Numata Center for Buddhist Translation, 2004.

Powers, John. "The Term 'Samdhinirmocana' in the Title of the Samdhinirmocana Sutra." *Studies in Central and East Asian Religions: Journal of the Seminar for Buddhist Studies,* Volume 4 (1992): 52–62.

Powers John, trans. *The Wisdom of Buddha: The Samdhinirmocana Mahayana Sutra.* Berkeley, CA: Dharma Publishing, 1995.

Red Pine. *The Diamond Sutra: Text and Commentaries Translated from Sanskrit and Chinese.* Berkeley, CA: Counterpoint, 2001.

———. *The Heart Sutra: Translation and Commentary.* Berkeley, CA: Counterpoint, 2004.

———. *The Lankavatara Sutra: A Translation and Commentary.* Berkeley, CA: Counterpoint, 2012.

Schopen, Gregory. *Figments and Fragments of Mahayana Buddhism in India.* Honolulu: University of Hawai'i Press, 2005.

Soeng, Mu. *Heart Sutra: Ancient Buddhist Wisdom in the Light of Quantum Reality.* Cumberland, RI: Primary Point Press, 1991.

Sparham, Gareth, trans. *Ocean of Eloquence: Tsong kha pa's Commentary on the Yogacara Doctrine of Mind.* Albany: State University of New York Press, 1993.

Thakchoe, Sonam. *The Two Truths Debate: Tsongkhapa and Gorampa on the Middle Way.* Boston: Wisdom, 2007.

Thrangu Rinpoche, Khenchen. *Everyday Consciousness and Buddha-Awakening.* Ithaca, NY: Snow Lion Publications, 2002.

Varela, Franscisco J., ed. *Sleeping, Dreaming, and Dying: An Exploration of Consciousness with the Dalai Lama.* Boston: Wisdom Publications, 1997.

Waldron, William. *The Buddhist Unconscious: The Alaya-Vijnana in the Context of Indian Buddhist Thought.* London: RoutledgeCurzon, 2003.

Index

About the Contributors

James William Coleman was born and raised in Southern California. He earned an MA and a PhD from the University of California, Santa Barbara, and is Professor of Sociology Emeritus at the California Polytechnic State University, San Luis Obispo, where he teaches the sociology of religion. His articles have been published in such places as *Buddhadharma*, the *American Journal of Sociology*, and the *Journal of Buddhist-Christian Studies*, and his books include *The New Buddhism: The Western Transformation of an Ancient Tradition*, published by Oxford University. He was also the editor of Reb Anderson Roshi's *The Third Turning of the Wheel: Wisdom of the Samdhinirmocana Sutra*. He has been a Buddhist practitioner in the Zen and Vajrayana traditions for over thirty years and is one of the founders of the White Heron Sangha in San Luis Obispo, California, where he currently teaches and practices. For more information or to contact the author see thebuddhasdream.net.

Reb Anderson Roshi is a lineage holder in the Soto Zen tradition and a senior Dharma teacher at the San Francisco Zen Center. Born in Mississippi, he grew up in Minnesota and came to the San Francisco Zen Center in 1967. He practiced with Suzuki Roshi, who ordained him as a priest in 1970 and gave him the name Tenshin Zenki ("Naturally Real, The Whole Works"). He received Dharma transmission in 1983 and served as abbot of San Francisco Zen Center's three training centers from 1986 to 1995. Tenshin Roshi continues to teach at the Zen Center and live at Green Gulch Farm. He is author of *Warm Smiles from Cold Mountains: Dharma Talks on Zen Meditation* and *Being Upright: Zen Meditation and the Bodhisattva Precepts* and *The Third Turning of the Wheel: Wisdom of the Samdhinirmocana Sutra.*

Lama Palden Drolma is the founder and spiritual director of Sukhasiddhi Foundation in Marin, California. She completed the traditional Tibetan Buddhist three-year retreat in the Shangpa and Karma Kagyu lineages under the previous Kalu Rinpoche's guidance in 1985. In 1986 she became one of the first Western women to be authorized as a lama in the Vajrayana tradition. In addition to Kalu Rinpoche, she has studied with many of the great Tibetan masters from all lineages, including the Sixteenth Gyalwa Karmapa, Tai Situ Rinpoche, Bokar Rinpoche, Jamgon Kongtrul Rinpoche, Khenpo Tsultrim Gyamtso Rinpoche, Dezhung Rinpoche, Dudjom Rinpoche, and the Dalai Lama.

Also Available from Wisdom Publications

Buddhism
One Teacher, Many Traditions
His Holiness the Dalai Lama and Thubten Chodron
Foreword by Bhante Gunaratana

"This book will reward those who study it carefully with a deep and wide understanding of the way these traditions have mapped their respective visions of the path to enlightenment."—Bhikkhu Bodhi, translator of *In the Buddha's Words*

Mindfulness in Plain English
Bhante Gunaratana

"A classic—one of the very best English sources for authoritative explanations of mindfulness."—Daniel Goleman, author of *Emotional Intelligence*

Zen Meditation in Plain English
John Daishin Buksbazen
Foreword by Peter Matthiessen

"A fine introduction to Zen meditation practice, grounded in tradition yet adapted to contemporary life."—*Publishers Weekly*

About Wisdom Publications

Wisdom Publications is the leading publisher of classic and contemporary Buddhist books and practical works on mindfulness. To learn more about us or to explore our other books, please visit our website at wisdompubs.org or contact us at the address below.

Wisdom Publications
199 Elm Street
Somerville, MA 02144 USA

We are a 501(c)(3) organization, and donations in support of our mission are tax deductible.

Wisdom Publications is affiliated with the Foundation for the Preservation of the Mahayana Tradition (FPMT).